Scammell and Densham

Law of Agricultural Holdings

Scammell and Densham
Law of Agricultural Holdings

Supplement to the eighth edition

HAC Densham
LLB, Solicitor of the Supreme Court

Della Evans
BA, LLM, Solicitor of the Supreme Court

Butterworths
London, Dublin, Edinburgh
2000

United Kingdom	Butterworths, a Division of Reed Elsevier (UK) Ltd, Halsbury House, 35 Chancery Lane, LONDON WC2A 1EL and 4 Hill Street, EDINBURGH EH2 3JZ
Australia	Butterworths, a Division of Reed International Books Australia Pty Ltd, CHATSWOOD, New South Wales
Canada	Butterworths Canada Ltd, MARKHAM, Ontario
Hong Kong	Butterworths Hong Kong, a division of Reed Elsevier (Greater China) Ltd, HONG KONG
India	Butterworths India, NEW DELHI
Ireland	Butterworth (Ireland) Ltd, DUBLIN
Malaysia	Malayan Law Journal Sdn Bhd, KUALA LUMPUR
New Zealand	Butterworths of New Zealand Ltd, WELLINGTON
Singapore	Butterworths Asia, SINGAPORE
South Africa	Butterworths Publishers (Pty) Ltd, DURBAN
USA	Lexis Law Publishing, CHARLOTTESVILLE, Virginia

© Reed Elsevier (UK) Ltd 2000

A CIP Catalogue record for this book is available from the British Library.

ISBN 0 406 91279 3

Typeset by M Rules
Printed and bound in Great Britain by Antony Rowe Ltd, Chippenham, Wilts

Visit Butterworths LEXIS *direct* **at www.butterworths.com**

Publisher's note

This Supplement to *Scammell and Densham's Law of Agricultural Holdings* covers legal developments since the eighth edition was published in 1997.

Among the recent cases dealt with in the Supplement, the important and radical decision of the House of Lords Decision in *Barrett v Morgan* has had a major effect on the security of sub-tenants and has wide ranging consequences for consensual notices to quit which are not confined to sub-tenancies. The Court of Appeal decisions in *Knipe v The National Trust* and *Floyer Acland v Osmond* have provided authoritative rulings on matters previously unlitigated.

This Supplement also considers a wide range of decisions by Tribunals and other inferior jurisdictions, which are of practical consequence for those engaged in the day to day operation of the agricultural holdings regime.

An update on general landlord and tenant law relevant to farm business tenancies is also included, along with a review of five years of the farm business tenancy regime.

November 2000

Contents

Contents

SECTION 1

Agricultural holdings under the Agricultural Holdings Act 1986

Chapter 1

Historical introduction

The page references in bold type in the left-hand margin are to page numbers in the main work.

The effect of Farm Business Tenancies upon protected tenancies

13 et seq Although the law applicable to tenancies created after 1 September 1995 falling within the Agricultural Tenancies Act 1995 has no application to tenancies protected under the Agricultural Holdings Act 1986, in practice the 1995 legislation has had a marked effect on tenancies falling within the 1986 Act regime. For example:

(a) Rent

There is now a real market in tenancies of farmland, ie Farm Business Tenancies. Although the rental formula applicable under the Agricultural Holdings Act 1986 is different from the open market formula applicable under the Agricultural Tenancies Act 1995, the effect of the open market upon the 1986 Act formula is having its effect.

The Court of Appeal in *Childers J W Trustees v Anker*[1] made a distinction between the market rent level applicable under the 1986 Act and an open market rental but did not define the distinction.

For further consideration of the inter-relationship of the two statutory régimes see noter-up to page 118, post.

(b) Security of tenure

The policy of the Agricultural Holdings Act 1986, like the 1948 Act before it, was to bring within security of tenure and within the definition of an agricultural holding most agreements, whether formal or informal, for the

1   [1996] 01 EG 102.

occupation of land by a farmer for the purposes of trade or business, subject only to very limited exceptions.

Since 1 September 1995 with the introduction of the legislation introduced by the Agricultural Tenancies Act 1995, public policy has been reversed. Now the statutory policy is to prevent such formal and informal arrangements from creating protected tenancies falling within the 1986 legislation, even when the parties expressly desire and attempt to contract into the 1986 regime.

In consequence, practitioners have found that the approach of the courts when considering long established arrangements for the occupation of farmland antedating the Agricultural Tenancies Act 1995, when considering whether in the absence of express agreement protected tenancies have been created falling within the Agricultural Holdings Act 1986, that the presumption in favour of the creation of a protected tenancy has, in practice, been reversed. Courts no longer readily assume the creation of a protected tenancy unless the landowner can establish otherwise with the heavy onus on the would-be tenant.

PART I

Formation of an agricultural holding

General introduction

17–24   Since all agricultural holdings falling within the definition of an 'agricultural holding' by section 1 of the Agricultural Holdings Act 1986 must have been created by an agreement entered into before 1 September 1995,[1] it follows that many of the exceptions to the definition of an agricultural holding are now spent. There can therefore be no extant:

(a) Grazing tenancies or licences falling within section 2 of the Agricultural Holdings Act 1986; or

42   (b) *Gladstone v Bower* agreements; or

43   (c) Ministry consent tenancies.

Any such purported tenancies created after 1 September 1995 either fall within the Agricultural Tenancies Act 1995 as Farm Business Tenancies or possibly within the Landlord and Tenant Act 1954, Pt II or else fall outside any statutory protected provision.

The security of sub-tenancies is even more precarious than was previously considered following the decision of the House of Lords in *Barrett v Morgan.*[2] In that case a tenant with a close community of interest with the landlord had inadvertently sublet to a third party. The landlord wished to

1   With the exceptions contained in section 4 of the Agricultural Tenancies Act 1995 as to which see the main work, page 906 et seq.
2   [2000] 2 WLR 284, [2000] 1 All ER 481.

recover possession. The fact that he as the head landlord gave notice to quit to the head tenant consensually, indeed, at the invitation of the tenant, did not convert the notice to quit into an agreement to surrender.

Accordingly, the effect of the notice to quit was to destroy the sub-tenancy and not to promote the sub-tenant to the status of protected tenant vis-à-vis the head landlord, as would have applied had the head tenancy been terminated by surrender.

For a further commentary on *Barrett v Morgan* and the position of sub-tenants generally, see the noter-up to pages 220–223.

Chapter 2

What is an agricultural holding?

A. AGRICULTURAL HOLDING

1. AGRICULTURAL LAND

(1) Land

27   *Blackmore v Butler* [1954] 1 QB 171
For later judicial opinion see *Tyack v Secretary of State for the Environment*[1] in which the House of Lords per Lord Bridge of Harwich expressed 'grave doubt' as to the correctness of the decision in *Blackmore v Butler* on the basis that it was not legitimate to treat the phrase 'used for agriculture' as equivalent to 'used in connection with agriculture' but did not overrule *Blackmore v Butler* in the absence of full argument as to the possible implications of the decision in the context of the Agricultural Holdings Acts.

(2) Used for agriculture

28   In *Floyer-Acland v Osmond*[2] the Court of Appeal decided, inter alia, that the reinstatement of land after gravel and sand extraction to full agricultural production by reinstatement of the topsoil, cultivating, seeding and even grazing, did not involve the use of the land for agriculture. It was work preparatory to such use as part of an aftercare condition. Therefore the land was not in agricultural use whilst the aftercare work was being undertaken. After paragraph (vi), insert a new paragraph:

(vii) See *Millington v Secretary of State for the Environment*[3] a case in which a farmer planted nine hectares as a vineyard and erected buildings for making wine. This was held to amount to the use of land for agriculture.

1   [1989] 1 WLR 1292, HL.
2   [2000] 22 EG 134, CA.
3   (1999) EGCS 95.

3

B. CHANGE OF STATUS

1. ABANDONMENT OF AGRICULTURAL USE

40   Footnote 2: Add *Russell v Booker* [1982] 263 EG 513 and *Hickson v Cann* [1977] 40 P & CR 218.

A. AGRICULTURAL HOLDING: SPECIAL FORMS

1. AGRICULTURAL HOLDINGS: NO SECURITY OF TENURE

(2) Ministry consent tenancies created before 1 September 1995 (two to five years)

44   *Pahl v Trevor*—see also *Jones v Owen*,[1] a case in which the court construed a ministry consent tenancy which was 'backdated' and yet excluded from security on application of the Court of Appeal provisions applied in *Pahl v Trevor*.

B. CONTRACTING OUT

67   An analagous but slightly different effect upon security of tenure was considered by the House of Lords in *Barrett v Morgan*.[2] In that case the head landlords and head tenant were closely connected parties. The head tenant had sublet inadvertently to the sub tenant. By agreement between the head landlord and the head tenant it was decided that the head landlord should serve notice to quit on the tenant, who would not serve a counternotice so that the head landlord could then recover possession from the sub tenant.

The House of Lords, reversing the decision of the Court of Appeal, decided that such a 'collusive' notice to quit was valid and effective for terminating the sub-tenancy. A landlord who was entitled to serve notice to quit unilaterally on his tenant effectively could also give such a notice consensually. It remained a notice to quit and did not become a surrender even though served with the consent and agreement of the tenant.

The case is to be distinguished from cases such as *Gisborne v Burton*[3] where the original letting and subletting were entered into as a means of creating a tenancy without security of tenure for the putative sub tenant. However, no such new tenancies since 1 September 1995 would come within the Agricultural Holdings Act 1986 in any event.

1   [1997] 32 EG 85.
2   [2000] 1 All ER 481, [2000] 2 WLR 284, HL.
3   [1989] QB 390.

For a discussion on the security of tenure available to sub tenants, see page 220 et seq of the main work, now heavily amended following the decision of the House of Lords in *Barrett v Morgan*.

PART II

The Tenancy Agreement: its terms and conditions

Chapter 5

Written tenancy agreement and fixed equipment

A. WRITTEN TENANCY AGREEMENT: SECTION 6 OF THE 1986 ACT

81   A problem which frequently arises in cases where a landlord has served a section 6 notice, but not pursued it further, is, how long it acts as a bar on assignment, subletting or parting with possession. A large number of section 6 notices were served soon after the passing of the Agricultural Holdings Act 1984 when the present wording of section 6 of the Agricultural Holdings Act 1986 was introduced.

Since the motivation for the service of the notice was to bar an assignment and there were, in reality, no other reasons for the giving of the notice or of securing of a written tenancy agreement, the notices have often been left on file. The question therefore arises as to when a tenant in such circumstances can proceed lawfully to assign on the basis that the notice has become time barred.

Section 6(5) and (6) only provide for the temporary barring of an assignment coming to an end in two specific circumstances:

(a) the conclusion of an agreement between the parties; or
(b) the making of an arbitrator's award.

Although the arbitration demanded can only be further activated by the landlord who had given the section 6 notice, the tenant can always prosecute the arbitration by giving his own notice under section 6. Therefore it is submitted that there is no statutory time barring other than as specifically contained in section 6(5) and (6) itself.

B. MAINTENANCE, REPAIR AND INSURANCE OBLIGATIONS: SECTION 7 OF THE 1986 ACT

THE 'MODEL CLAUSES'

84   NB In the eighth edition, page 845, the notes to a Notice to Remedy in Form 2 which is frequently used to enforce compliance by the tenant with the Model Clauses obligations, are incomplete: paragraph 4 of the notes is missing important words including paragraph (b). For the full text see noter-up to page 845, post.

E. TENANT'S RIGHT TO REMOVE FIXTURES AND BUILDINGS: SECTION 10

93   *TSB v Botham*[1]: and see also *Elitestone Limited v Morris*.[2]

F. PROVISION OF FIXED EQUIPMENT

1. CONDITIONS FOR DIRECTION OF THE AGRICULTURAL LAND TRIBUNAL TO THE LANDLORD

96   For examples of tribunal decisions in which directions have been made against landlords requiring them to undertake pollution control measures, see *Hindle v Wright and Ahmed re: Knuzden Moss Pigeries near Blackburn Lancs* (ALT Western Area) and *Sutcliffe v Lawrenson re: Laithwaite Farm, Cockram, Lancs* (ALT Western Area).

---

1   [1995] ECGS 3.
2   [1997] 27 EG 116.

CHAPTER 6

Rent review and distress

A. GENERAL RENT REVIEW

2. PROCEDURE

(1) The trigger notice

103   After paragraph (b) insert:

(c) A further problem frequently encountered on which there is as yet no authority, is whether one of two or more joint landlords can serve notice under section 12 and then pursue a rent review without the concurrence (or even in the face of actual hostility) of the other landlord(s). This problem often arises when one of the landlords is also a (or the) tenant who therefore wishes to resist any rent increase. On the face of it one of two or more landlords holds as a trustee who can only act jointly with the other landlord(s).

It is submitted that: (i) the definition of 'landlord' in section 96 includes 'any' and is not confined to 'all', cf *Parsons v Parsons*[1] which was not concerned with the exercise of a statutory right; (ii) 'the doctrine of joint participation by joint tenants is not a sacrosanct or immutable doctrine of statutory interpretation' (per Buxton LJ in *De Rothschild v Bell*.[2] The court must look at the purpose of the legislation in order to decide whether a joint tenant or joint landlord is entitled to claim the benefit of rights conferred on the joint tenancy by that enactment. See also *Leek and Morlands Building Society v Clark*.[3]

3. THE VALUATION FORMULA

(1) The amount of rent: the rent properly payable

109   Frequently the greatest problem in anticipating the rent level to be awarded by an arbitrator and therefore the level at which to settle and avoid the expense and uncertainty of an arbitration is that the factors to be taken into account in arriving at the rent properly payable pull in different directions. The rent which would be appropriate having regard 'to the productive capacity' and 'the related earning capacity' suggest an affordable rent which could be funded from the profit earned from working the farm.

By contrast, the rent 'at which the holding might reasonably be expected to be let . . .' suggests market rent (albeit not an open market rent per

1   [1993] 1 WLR 1390.
2   [1999] 16 EG 155.
3   [1952] 2 QB 788.

Childers v Anker). The rent to be arrived at by reference to comparable rents, again may well pull in a different direction. There is no guidance as to how the arbitrator is to reconcile or apply those different figures in determining the rent eventually selected and no guidance will be provided by the court (see per Forbes J in *Estates Projects Limited v Greenwich London Borough* cited on page 99 of the main work).

In consequence, provided the arbitrator takes into account the competing factors in awarding the rent properly payable, his award will be unchallengable. Therefore, there is no 'right' answer to the question as to what is the rent properly payable. Considerable discretion is afforded to the individual arbitrators to select the rent to be awarded from the range of figures provided by the factors which fall to be taken into account but none of which is determinative.

(2) Factors to be taken into account

(d) Comparables

(iv) Types of comparable

118   For cases since *Spath Holme Ltd v Greater Manchester and Lancashire Rent Assessment Committee*[1] see *Northumberland and Durham Property Trust v London Rent Assessment Committee*[2] and *BTE Ltd v Merseyside and Cheshire RAC*[3] *and Curtis v Chairwoman of the London Rent Assessment Committee.*[4]

It is always dangerous to apply principles laid down under a different landlord and tenant regime such as the Rent Acts and the Housing Act and to apply those to a different legislative procedure, ie in this context the Agricultural Holdings Act 1986. However, pending a decision of the courts on the application of the principles applied in those cases to agricultural holdings, it is submitted that for an arbitrator to reject evidence of farm business tenancy rents of otherwise comparable holdings on the basis that they are inadmissible would probably amount to an error of law on the part of the arbitrator.

Therefore it is probable that the Court of Appeal's ruling that in the light of the growing volume of market rents they are 'the natural successors to the declining regime of registered fair rents'[5] and similar rulings will apply to agricultural holdings, in providing the best evidence from which a 1986 rent is to be derived. When considering the comparable phenomenon in the context of dwellinghouses the court had decided that in cases where there are sufficient market rent comparables available 'there is normally no need to refer to registered fair rent comparables at all. It follows that to rely in such circumstances on registered fair rents whether generally or particularly unless one or other party can dislodge them as suitable comparables, is wrong'[5].

1   [1995] 2 EGLR 80.
2   [1997] 1 EGLR 236.
3   [1992] 1 EGLR 116.
4   [1997] EGCS 132.
5   *Spath Holme Ltd v Greater Manchester and Lancashire Rent Assessment Committee* [1995] 2 EGLR 80.

In determining whether rents assessed under farm business tenancies are admissible, the first question for consideration is whether a letting of a farm business tenancy falling within the Agricultural Tenancies Act 1986 is a letting of 'an agricultural holding'. If so, the second question is whether the particular farm business tenancy which is produced as a comparable to the subject holding was let on 'terms (other than terms fixing the rent payable) similar to those of the tenancy under consideration . . .'.

It is submitted in answer:

(a) Although by definition a farm business tenancy does not enjoy any security of tenure, nevertheless with very few exceptions farm business tenancies will come within the definition of an agricultural holding contained in sections 1 and 96 of the 1986 Act because they will satisfy the definition of a 'contract for an agricultural tenancy'.

(b) For the terms to be 'similar' does not require them to be 'identical'. It is probable that the court will adopt a fairly wide definition relying upon the ability to evaluate and adjust for incomparable features rather than exclude such evidence entirely.

PART III

Security of Tenure

Chapter 9

Notices to quit: general rules

B. VALIDITY OF NOTICE TO QUIT

1. THE TERM DATE

157   *Mannai Investments Co Ltd v Eagle Star Life Assurance Co Ltd* has now been the subject of an appeal to the House of Lords.[1] Until now the courts have been inconsistent in their approach to the need for accuracy in notices to quit. The House of Lords decision has now explained and simplified the law. It overruled the decision in *Hankey v Clavering*[2] (cited at footnote 4 of the main work) and decided that the real question that fell to be answered in individual cases was 'Is the notice quite clear to a reasonable tenant reading it? Is it plain that he cannot be misled by it?'. In the *Mannai* case itself the tenant had served a break clause in a lease and inadvertently had specified the wrong date. He was one day out. It was held that this was not misleading and his intention was clear and therefore the notice was valid. For cases in which serious and major errors

---

1   [1997] 1 EGLR 57.
2   [1942] 2 KB 326.

have been excused from invalidating the notices in which the errors occurred see footnote 4 to page 157 and footnote 7 to page 159 in the main work.

3. ACCURACY: STRICT OR LIBERAL CONSTRUCTION

157/158   Footnote 5 page 157 and footnote 5 page 158:
In the light of the authoritative ruling of the House of Lords in *Mannai Investments Co Ltd* (supra) *Hankey v Clavering* has been overruled and the law as set out in *Carradine Properties Ltd* (supra) and *Germax Securities Ltd* (supra) correctly states the law as it now is.

159   After line 13, insert:

4. NOTICE TO QUIT: WITHOUT PREJUDICE

In *Grammer v Lane*[1] there was a dispute as to whether or not a land owner had created an agricultural holding in favour of the farmer who was claiming a tenancy. The landlord gave notice to revise the rent under section 12 'without prejudice' to his contention that there was no existing tenancy at all. He similarly gave a notice to remedy breaches. Thereafter he sought the appointment of an arbitrator in each case. Concurrently the 'tenant' issued proceedings for a declaration that he held a tenancy.

It was held that there was 'no reason in principle why a freeholder could not serve a notice or take relevant arbitrarial steps pending the resolution of an outstanding dispute as to whether any tenancy existed at all. The scheme of the Act was not "flouted".'

5. PROTECTION FROM EVICTION ACT 1977 – SECTION 5: *NATIONAL TRUST V KNIPE*[2]

After a period of uncertainty the Court of Appeal has decided, reversing the judge at first instance, that a notice to quit given in respect of an agricultural holding which included a dwellinghouse does not have to comply with section 5 of the Protection from Eviction Act 1977. The prescribed information would be either misleading or irrelevant in the case of an agricultural holding.

1   [2000] 04 EG 135.
2   [1997] 40 EG 151.

Period of Notice

161/162   After paragraph (ii) insert:

(iii)   Although there is no authority on this matter, it is submitted that if there is an express provision and not merely the statutory requirement that 12 months' notice must be given to terminate the tenancy, then even though eg the tenant becomes insolvent (section 25(2)(a)), the landlord could not give a six months' notice. This is because section 25(2)(a) merely overrides the general provision that 12 months' notice must be given notwithstanding any lesser period provided for in the tenancy agreement. It does not override a contractual extension of the common law six months rule to twelve months.

CHAPTER 11

Incontestable notices to quit: the 'seven deadly sins'

B. GENERAL PRINCIPLES

3. STRICT CONSTRUCTION

179   Since the decision of the Court of Appeal in *Pickard v Bishop* there has been a marked change in the judicial approach to the strictness to be complied when construing documents. See *Mannai Investments Co Ltd v Eagle Star Life Assurance Co Ltd*[1] overriding *Hankey v Clavering*.[2] However, that case and that line of authorities did not address notices with what was described as penal consequences such as forfeiture notices and notices served under Case D of Schedule 3 to the Agricultural Holdings Act 1986, which carry with them draconian consequences for non-compliance. It is submitted that the line of cases including *Pickard v Bishop, Dickinson v Boucher* et al, still apply to such notices to pay or notices to remedy.

4. DEMAND FOR ARBITRATION MANDATORY

180   A formal, or indeed an informal, letter which makes it clear that the tenant wishes to dispute the validity of the reasons stated for the giving of a notice must also say that he demands arbitration. It is insufficient merely to make it clear that the tenant challenges the landlord's notice to quit: *Rous v Mitchell*.[3]

1   [1997] 24 EG 122.
2   [1942] 2 KB 326.
3   [1991] 1 All ER 676.

181   after line 5 insert:

What is compulsorily referable to arbitration?

The combined effect of article 9 of the Agricultural Holdings (Arbitration on Notices) Order 1987 and the decision in *Magdalen College Oxford v Heritage* and the other cases cited above is that it is only 'the reason stated for the giving of the notice to quit' in question which has to be compulsorily referable to arbitration. If therefore the tenant wishes to challenge another aspect of the notice to quit, for example, as to whether it relates to the whole of the holding or is invalid as a notice to quit part only without an available ground for such a notice or as to whether the notice was duly served or generally as to the common law validity of the notice, then there is no requirement that the tenant should give a counter-notice demanding arbitration. He is entitled to raise his defence when the landlord seeks an order for possession or declaration as to the validity of the notice given. The tenant is not inhibited from raising such matters not falling within the meaning of 'the reasons stated for the giving of the notice to quit'. What is less clear is the extent of the arbitrator's jurisdiction to determine matters not confined simply to the reasons stated. It is submitted that on parity of reasoning with the decision of the Court of Appeal is *Kirby* v *Robinson*,[1] that the test is whether the matter being raised is so inextricably a part of the reasons stated that the arbitrator must or would find it desirable to determine the other matter in fulfilling his duties to determine the reasons stated. If so, his jurisdiction would extend to include a determination on such other matter extending beyond what is confined to the reasons stated for the notice itself. See also *Crawley v Pratt*[2] in which a tenant failed to demand arbitration but challenged a Case B notice because it allegedly related to part only of the holding. The Court of Appeal decided that on its true construction the notice related to the whole holding therefore it was valid even though only part was required for non-agricultural purposes. Had the reasons stated been referred to arbitration then the notice to quit would almost certainly have failed.

2. CASE B—PLANNING CONSENT: NON-AGRICULTURAL USE

184   See *Floyer-Acland v Osmond*,[3] in which a landlord who had obtained planning permission to extract sand and gravel from part of a holding, gave notice to quit under Case B. When the tenant challenged the notice, the landlord gave notice to re-enter in reliance upon the reservation of mines and minerals contained in the tenancy agreement. It was held:

1   [1965] 195 EG 363.
2   [1988] 2 EGLR 6, CA.
3   [2000] 22 EG 134.

(a) That he could nevertheless pursue the notice to quit and the land was still 'required'. He did not need to show that he needed to terminate the tenancy, merely that he wanted to do so in addition to exercising the reservation. He was not put on his election.

(b) The aftercare condition requiring reinstatement of the land, cultivation of the reinstated soil, seeding and then grazing, was not agricultural use but work of preparation for later agricultural use which did not invalidate the notice. Therefore the use proposed by the landlord was still 'otherwise than for agriculture' even though the non-agricultural use was temporary.

(c) Concurrent agricultural and non-agricultural uses would have been fatal to the validity of the notice. Therefore if land is to be used for example for keeping and breeding horses (non-agricultural) and for grazing (whether by horses or agricultural animals, ie livestock) that will invalidate the notice.

NB The distinction between needing the land and simply wanting it should not be confused with need for a bona fide intention which is required. The landlord must have a genuine intention to use the land for the specified non-agricultural use even though it is not necessary, still less essential, that the notice to quit is upheld.

185   Footnote 5:
In addition to *Omnivale v Bolden,* see *Crawley v Pratt* [1988] 2 EGLR 6.

186   After paragraph (g) (which starts on page 186) insert:
Frequently, a landlord giving notice to quit in reliance upon Case B will also rely upon a short notice provision in the tenancy agreement (see section 25(2)(b) page 160 ante).

If the tenant then gives a counter-notice demanding arbitration, the effect of the demand will be to postpone the operation of the notice to quit (see SI 1987/710).

The consequence is that the distinction between a short notice and a full 12 months' notice is eroded and often extinguished altogether.

3. CASE C—CERTIFICATE OF BAD HUSBANDRY

187   *Goodwin v Clarke*[1]
Where a landlord had applied for a certificate of bad husbandry and before the hearing, on inspection, had discovered that the breaches committed previously by the tenant had been remedied, it was held that since the landlord did not withdraw his application for a certificate, by continuing with the litigation he was then guilty of 'vexatious, frivolous or oppressive' behaviour and as such was liable for the costs of the tenant from that time onwards.

1   Decision of the Eastern Area ALT [1992] EA 605.

For a similar decision of an Agricultural Land Tribunal (Yorkshire and Humberside) in the case of a succession case see *Clappison v Marr Trustees*.

4. CASE D—NON-COMPLIANCE WITH NOTICE TO PAY RENT, OR NOTICE TO REMEDY A BREACH OF THE TENANCY

(1) Non-payment of rent after notice to pay

190 Insert at the end of paragraph (e):
A notice to pay or a notice to remedy must be in the prescribed form and must include the notes which form part of the notice in each case. For a decision as to the effect of the notes upon the validity of the notice see *Bolton (House Furnishers) v Oppenheim*.[1]

190 Insert new paragraph (ff):
Payment of rent by leaving a cheque in the dairy is insufficient because that is not a proper method of payment (see *Flint v Fox*[2]). Service of a notice by leaving a notice at the farmhouse where it was slipped under the floor and even the linoleum where it remained undetected, was held to be sufficient (*Newborough v Jones*[3]).

192 Line 1 delete 'or' and substitute 'and'.

193 Footnote 5: see also *Mannai* supra ('benign' does not mean re-writing).

197 and *a. What breaches are remediable and what are irremediable?*
205 Although there has been little authority specifically in the context of the Agricultural Holdings Act 1986 and notices to quit, a distinction between remediable and irremediable breaches has been extensively researched and discussed by the Court of Appeal in the context of forfeiture proceedings and section 146 of the Law of Property Act 1925. See *Savva v Hussein*[4] and the earlier decision of Mummery J at first instance in *Bilson v Residential Apartments Ltd.*[5] Though this case was the subject of an appeal, the Court of Appeal did not consider the first instance decision on the distinction between remediable and irremediable breaches.
The present state of the law would therefore appear to be as follows:

(a) Breach of a prohibition upon assignment and subletting which is specifically found to be incapable of remedy is retained as a special case (per Storton LJ in *Savva v Hussein* at page 154).

1   [1959] 1 WLR 913.
2   [1956] 106 LJ 928.
3   [1975] Ch 9.
4   [1997] 73 P & CR 150.
5   [1990] 60 P & CR 392.

(b) Breach of other prohibitions, eg upon the making of alterations without the landlord's prior consent, by definition cannot be remedied. 'However if the mischief caused by the breach can be removed' then the breach is said to be capable of remedy by that process. 'In the case of a covenant not to make alterations without consent or not to display signs without consent, if there is a breach of that the mischief can be removed by removing the signs or restoring the property to the state it was in before the alterations' (ibid).

(c) There is nothing 'in logic which requires different considerations between a positive and a negative covenant . . . the test is one of effect. If a breach has been remedied then it must have been capable of being remedied'.

(d) The contrary view expressed by Mummery J in *Bilson* (supra) was disapproved of. Mummery J had held that where the tenant made alterations to the property in breach where there was a condition requiring the landlord's consent to be obtained first before any alterations were made, he had held 'Now that the alterations had been made without consent it is impossible for the defendants to comply with the covenant which required them first to apply for consent . . . In those circumstances I hold that the breach was not capable of remedy'. That would not appear to be a correct statement of the law as now understood.

(e) In the case of a notice to quit under Case E relying upon an irremediable breach, in any event the landlord has the additional hurdle of having to prove 'that at the date of the giving of the notice to quit the interest of the landlord in the agricultural holding has been materially prejudiced' by reason of the breach. It is submitted therefore that even those breaches which are said to be incapable of remedy, cannot effectively found a Case E Notice to quit if the tenant is able to return to the pre-existing status because then 'the mischief resulting from a breach of the covenant can be removed'. See Stourton LJ in *Savva* (supra).

See also in this context *Rous v Mitchell*[1] and the commentary at page 210 footnote 1 of the main work.

(f) Breach of a prohibition on assigning, sub-letting or parting with possession are subject to their own special circumstances for the reasons explained in *Scala House and District Property Co Ltd v Forbes*[2] and extensions by analogy to other breaches of covenant are unlikely to be upheld.

198   Footnote 1:
See also *Savva v Hussein* (supra) and the noter-up to page 197.

1   [1991] 1 All ER 676.
2   [1974] QB 575.

7. CASE G—THE DEATH OF THE TENANT

212   Footnote 1:
Note: The appeal to the Court of Appeal in *Walton v Buckminster Estate* was discontinued.

Paragraph (e) insert:

213   For the form of application to the Public Trustee for registration of notice affecting land to which the Public Trustee (Notices Affecting Land) (Title on Death) Regulations 1995 apply, see post, page 853.

Chapter 12

Miscellaneous provisions regarding notices to quit

A. NOTICE TO QUIT PART

4. REDUCTION OF RENT AFTER NOTICE TO QUIT PART

219   Note: Contrary to what is stated in the work, a variation in the rent by a reduction following resumption of possession of part of the holding in either of the circumstances referred to in section 33(1) will *not* start time running afresh for the three year rent review provisions. This applies whether the rent reduction is occasioned by arbitration or by agreement.

B. SUB-TENANTS

1. NOTICE TO QUIT

220   It has now been authoritatively determined by the House of Lords (reversing the decision of the Court of Appeal) in *Barrett v Morgan*[1] that a notice to quit remains a notice to quit and is not to be treated as the equivalent of a surrender agreement even where the head landlord gives to the head tenant a notice to quit by agreement and, indeed, at the invitation of the head tenant so as to affect the destruction by operation of law of the sub-tenancy.

As a landlord can give notice to quit unilaterally without the concurrence of the tenant, so the notice to quit does not cease to be a notice to quit merely because the tenant agrees to the landlord taking the action he is entitled to take in any event, even without the concurrence of the tenant. The

---

1   [2000] 2 WLR 284, [2000] 1 All ER 481.

addition of the pejorative adjective 'collusive' to an agreement does not change the nature of the transaction since all agreements are consensual by their nature and therefore, collusive.

221 Paragraph (d) (ii) penultimate line:
Delete 'The head tenant has not . . .' and substitute 'the sub-tenant has not . . .'.

2. SURRENDER, FORFEITURE AND OTHER METHODS OF TERMINATION

222 Footnotes 3 and 4:
It is doubtful whether in the light of the House of Lords decision in *Barrett v Morgan* (supra) that the decision in *Cowen v Tanner*[1] would be followed today. In that case a distinction was made between forfeiture by the unilateral action of the landlord without the concurrence of the head tenant and forfeiture with the co-operation of the head tenant who signed a consent order so as to save the further costs of the litigation in the erroneous belief that there was no sustainable defence. On parity of reasoning with the House of Lords decision in *Barrett v Morgan*, the termination of the head tenancy by forfeiture which thereby also destroyed the sub-tenancy remained a termination by forfeiture and was not converted into a quasi-surrender because of the consent to the order for possession by the head tenant in the circumstances applicable in that case.

It would now appear to be the law that it is only where there is a termination of the head tenancy by a surrender properly so-called consensually between head landlord and head tenant that the sub tenancy is preserved and is not destroyed by operation of law on the termination of the head tenancy out of which the sub-tenancy was carved or created. Other methods of termination, even though agreed upon consensually between head landlord and head tenant, will destroy the sub-tenancy.

1   [1900] 2 QB 609.

PART IV

Succession on death or retirement of tenant

Chapter 14

Succession on death

A. TENANCIES WITH AND WITHOUT SUCCESSION RIGHTS

4. TWO PREVIOUS SUCCESSIONS: SECTION 37 OF THE 1986 ACT

243

Insert at the end of paragraph (c):
Succession by assignment can be effected even when succession by determination and regrant is not possible. This is because an assignment succession can operate for a tenancy granted to joint tenants where only one satisfies the requirements of section 37(2) as being a close relative of the previous tenant. Furthermore, such assignee does not need to have satisfied the other tests of eligibility or of suitability. The close relationship test alone has to have been satisfied. It should further be remembered that between 1976 with the passing of the Agriculture (Miscellaneous Provisions) Act 1976 and 12 September 1984, succession could only be effected by the grant of a new tenancy and not by assignment.

Insert at the end of paragraph (e):
Note that the decision of Jowitt J obiter in *Saunders v Ralph* to the effect that an inter vivos succession even before 1976 could operate as a succession for the purposes of applying the two succession rule, has been criticised by commentators but not judicially. On the other hand, his ratio that the addition of a second tenant as a joint tenant could be operated by a variation of the tenancy and not by the operation of the fiction of surrender and re-grant would appear to be in line with current judicial thinking and the more authoritative decision of the Court of Appeal in *Childers v Anker*.[1]

Footnote 1:
For a case in which an individual Agricultural Land Tribunal has decided that work undertaken by an applicant as a contractor on land away from the holding, nevertheless fell to be treated as qualifying agricultural work on the holding, see *Sandercock v Sandercock*.[2]

1   [1996] 1 EG 102, CA.
2   [2000] ALT Midlands Area.

251   After line 6 insert:

B. QUALIFICATIONS FOR SUCCESSION

1. ELIGIBLE PERSONS: SECTIONS 35, 36 AND 41 AND SCHEDULE 6 TO THE 1986 ACT

(3) The principal source of livelihood test: sections 36(3)(a) and 41, and Part I of Schedule 6, paragraph 2

(a) Applicant fully eligible

(i) Agricultural work

For a case in which a Tribunal had to consider whether income derived from quota leasing where a dairy farming enterprise had been discontinued and both the milk quota and sheep quota was leased out, was qualifying income, see *Sandercock v Sandercock*.[1] The Tribunal decided 'the source of the quota rents was immaterial. The proper consideration was how the applicant had access to them. Once they had gone into the partnership account the only reason he was able to draw on them was because what he drew was in recognition of his agricultural work on the unit of which the holding formed part. He was economically dependent on that unit. His agricultural work on that unit was the source of almost the whole of his livelihood, certainly well over 50%'.

(4) Commercial unit occupation test

(a) Commercial unit of agricultural land

256   Insert after the words at the end of paragraph 2 'the Agricultural Holdings (Units of Production) Order 1996' the words 'and now the Agricultural Holdings (Units of Production) (England) Order 2000'.
       Following the enactment of the Government of Wales Act 1998 and the consequent devolution of certain central government functions to an elected Assembly of Wales it is probable that a new set of concurrent Units of Production Order applicable only to Wales will be made. Currently no such Order of equivalent provision has been made and for the time being the current regulations applicable to England will also apply to Wales.

258   After sub-paragraph (vii) insert a new sub-paragraph:
       (viii) The practice of the Ministry of Agriculture has been to publish statistical average evidence of the 'the aggregate of the average annual earnings of full time male agricultural workers aged 20 or over'

---

1   [2000] ALT Midlands Area.

quarterly, thereby mirroring the wording of para 3(1) of Schedule 6 to the Agricultural Holdings Act 1986. These figures have been widely used by Agricultural Land Tribunals as the relevant figures to be compared with the figures produced by the Agricultural Holdings (Units of Production) figures in determining the notional income available from the holding. This practice has now been discontinued. In the absence of available statistical information, considerable difficulties are presented to individual litigants and Tribunals.

(b) The occupation tests

(i) Non-disqualifying occupation

258/259   The 'non-disqualifying occupations' referred to in paragraphs a. to e. inclusive, are now all spent by reason of the passing of the Agricultural Tenancies Act 1995. These are all contained in Schedule 6, para 6(1) (a) to (d) inclusive. However, those referred to in paras (dd), (e) and (f) of Schedule 6 remain of paramount importance.

h. Farm business tenancies

260   Under **para 6(1)(dd)** referred to in the main work at **page 260 para h**, the form of farm business tenancy which falls to be excluded as an occupation disregarded for the purposes of the occupancy condition, is a farm business tenancy 'for less than five years (including a farm business tenancy which is a periodic tenancy)', the words used are not for a fixed term of which less than five years remain unexpired. Therefore it would appear that where the applicant occupies under a farm business tenancy which was granted for a term of five years or more, even though less than five years remains unexpired, then the farm business tenancy does not fall to be disregarded and the applicant's occupation must be taken into account in determining whether he falls to be rendered ineligible as the occupier of a commercial unit.

2. SUITABLE PERSONS

264   Footnote 2:

When considering the standard by which an applicant's suitability is to be assessed, a further difficulty has been introduced by the steep decline in farming profitability due to the reduction in the value, or at least the prices paid, for most forms of farm production. For an example of an applicant who was a casualty of declining farming profitability, see *R W Cant v British Steel Plc*.[1]

1   EA 861 12.11.1998.

PART V

Compensation on quitting

Chapter 16

The tenant's claims on quitting: general

B. COMPENSATION FOR IMPROVEMENTS

2. NEW IMPROVEMENTS

(1) Rules for entitlement to compensation

327   Para (a):
For a recent case in which the Agricultural Land Tribunal considered and granted consent for an improvement with an open ended compensation provision and where the landlord was only prepared to give consent subject to a write-off for compensation, see *Barton v Lincolnshire Trust for Nature Conservancy*.[1]

In that case it was agreed that the construction of an eight million gallon irrigation reservoir to catch winter rainfall on tenanted land in Lincolnshire, was desirable but the landlord argued that the Trust needed to know what its accumulated liability was and therefore a write-off in that case proposed of 20 years was necessary to avoid criticism by the Charity Commission.

The Tribunal decided that any condition or write off would not be justified and that compensation should be payable in accordance with section 66(1) of the Agricultural Holdings Act 1986 particularly since the value of the improvement at the end of the tenancy 'cannot be guessed before that time comes'.

Chapter 17

The tenant's claims on quitting: milk quota

A. GENERAL INTRODUCTION

342   Add to footnote 1:
Council Regulation 3950/92 establishing an additional levy in the milk

---

1   [1997] ALT; Eastern Area EA 817.

and milk products sector and Council Regulation 536/93 laying down detailed rules on the additional levy on milk and milk products.

Add to footnote 2:
These regulations currently in force are the Dairy Produce Quota Regulations 1997, SI 1997/733 (as amended by SIs 1997/1093 and 2000/699 and 2000/972).

343   Add to footnote 2:
The current regulations are the Milk Quota (Calculation of Standard Quota) Order 1992, SI 1992/1225.

Line 31:
Re *R v MAFF, ex p Bostock*: The case proceeded to the European Court by way of a reference for a preliminary ruling in the course of an application to the English court for judicial review.

B. ENTITLEMENT TO COMPENSATION

1. PREREQUISITES FOR ENTITLEMENT

345   The machinery for allocation by the Minister of Agriculture was not via the Milk Marketing Board at the time of the original allocation in 1984.

346   Line 9:
Delete 'Eckroyd' and substitute 'Ecroyd'.

2. RELEVANT QUOTA

Last line:
The regulations currently in force are the Dairy Produce Quota Regulations 1997, SI 1997/733 (as amended by SIs 1997/1093 and 2000/699 and 2000/972.

C. ASSESSMENT OF COMPENSATION

1. TRANSFERRED QUOTA

347   Footnote 3:
The current regulations are the Milk Quota (Calculation of Standard Quota) (Amendment) Order 1992, SI 1992/1225.

Footnote 7:
The regulations currently in force are the Dairy Produce Quota Regulations 1997, SI 1997/733 (as amended by 1997/1093 and 2000/699 and 2000/972).

2. EXCESS OVER STANDARD QUOTA

(1) The 'normal case'

348   Footnote 5:
The current regulations are the Milk Quota (Calculation of Standard Quota) (Amendment) Order 1992, SI 1992/1225.

349   Footnote 8:
The current regulations are the Milk Quota (Calculation of Standard Quota) (Amendment) Order 1992, SI 1992/1225.

350   Add to footnote 3:
See now *Elitstone Ltd v Morris* [1997] 2 All ER 513.

351   Footnote 4:
The current regulations are the Milk Quota (Calculation of Standard Quota) (Amendment) Order 1992, SI 1992/1225.

D. VALUATION OF THE CLAIM: SCHEDULE 1, PARAGRAPH 9

356   ## 1. THE LEGALITY OF THE UK MILK QUOTA TRANSFER SYSTEM

(a) The Dairy Produce Quotas Regulations 1997, SI 1997/733 (particularly reg 7 and Sch 2) now specifically authorise the practice which had become the normal method of affecting a milk quota transfer by means of a short term change of occupation of land.

    The Court of Appeal has now authoritatively determined also that the UK milk quota transfer system as practised by way of a short term grazing tenancy is valid and effective. See *Harries v Barclays Bank*[1] and particularly the judgment of Morritt LJ at 18.

(b) The nature of milk quota and its legal status in UK law has been extensively considered particularly in *Faulks v Faulks*,[2] *Davies v Ecroyd*[3] and by the Court of Appeal in *Harries* (supra). The conclusion

---

1   [1997] 2 EGLR 14.
2   [1992] 15 EG 82.
3   [1996] 30 EG 7.

that milk quota is not an asset separate and distinct from the holding in relation to which it was or becomes registered has been challenged by the High Court decision in *Swift v Dairywise Farms Ltd*[1] (which is itself currently under consideration by the Court of Appeal). Also see *Cottle v Caldicott*[2].

(c) For cases in which the court has considered the nature, extent and circumstances of changes of occupation giving rise to transfer of milk quota see also *R v MAFF, ex p Cox*[3] and *Holdcroft v Staffordshire County Council*.[4]

(d) Milk quota can now be transferred without any change of occupation of the land to which the quota is 'attached' by virtue of SI 1997/733, reg 11. There are restrictions which do not apply to transfers of quota with land which have proved to be a serious restraint upon the use of this method of transfer.

Chapter 20

Settlement of claims made on quitting

DISPUTES PROCEDURE

2. STATUTORY PROCEDURES

(2) Subsequent steps for enforcement of claims

382   A problem which often arises is as to whether the parties are obliged to wait the full eight month period specified in section 83 before an application can be made for the appointment of an arbitrator. The problem is often particularly acute in the context of milk quota compensation claims where there may be substantial sums at issue. The landlord will have had the whole of the milk quota, including the transferred quota, transferred to him on termination of the tenancy and the tenant will receive no compensation unless and until agreement has been reached between the parties or an arbitrator's award has been made.

Furthermore, the arbitrator's award only carries interest from the date specified by the arbitrator, which must be after the date of the award (see para 2 of Sch 11 of the Agricultural Holdings Act 1986).

Section 83(1) provides a mandatory requirement for any dispute to be determined by arbitration. Section 83(4) provides that the parties may, within eight months from the termination of the tenancy, settle by agreement and section 83(5) provides that there must be determination by arbitration after the expiration of the eight month period. There is, however, nothing to

1   [2000] 1 All ER 320.
2   [1995] STC 239.
3   [1993] 1 EGLR 17.
4   [1994] 2 EGLR 1.

prevent either party seeking the appointment of an arbitrator before the eight month period has expired. The parties are not obliged to await the expiration of the eight month period before an application can be made for the appointment of an arbitrator, and the paying party (landlord for milk quota, for example, but tenant for dilapidation claims likewise) may not therefore postpone his liability to pay without interest or cost penalties.

PART VI

Disputes procedures and miscellaneous

C. THE ARBITRATION PROCEDURES

3. THE AWARD

(4) Costs

412   For a case in which a county court judge opined that the arbitrator had no power to exercise a lien on his award until his costs had been paid but the matter was not argued on that issue, see *Sloane Stanley Estate Trustees v Barribal*.[1] The matter did not arise in the Court of Appeal where the substantive judgment was reversed.

Chapter 22

Agricultural Land Tribunals and the courts

A. AGRICULTURAL LAND TRIBUNALS

3. PROCEDURE

(7) Costs

425/426   The unrestricted power of the Agricultural Land Tribunal to order the payment of costs by any party in proceedings not confined to an Order against a party who had acted 'frivolously, vexatiously or oppressively' introduced by section 27(7) of the 1986 Act *only* applies to 'proceedings under this section', ie proceedings brought under section 27 itself.

---

1   [1994] 2 EGLR 8, [1994] 44 EG 237, CA.

An application to the Agricultural Land Tribunal for consent to the operation of a notice to quit are not proceedings brought 'under this section' but under section 26. Section 27 sets out matters on which the Tribunal has to be satisfied before giving consent, not under section 27 but under section 26.

B. THE COURTS

429   For a case in which the Court of Appeal recently considered the inter-relationship between the jurisdiction of the courts and the concurrent jurisdictions of arbitrators and where notices had been given to a 'tenant' without prejudice to the land owner's contention and submission that there was no subsisting tenancy in place at all which was the subject of declaratory relief sought by the would-be tenant in the court legislation, see *Grammar v Lane.*[1] In that case it was held that it was permissible for a landowner, whilst denying the subsistence of a tenancy at all, to give notice to remedy breaches and to demand arbitration as to the rent in each case 'without prejudice' to the primary submission that no tenancy had ever been created in the first place.

Chapter 23

Miscellaneous provisions

D. SERVICE OF NOTICES

SECTION 93

(2) Service by post: registered post and recorded delivery

438   Footnote 1:
Practice Direction [1968] 3 All ER 319 has now been superseded by *Practice Direction* [1985] 1 All ER 889.

(4) Service by facsimile and e-mail

439   Service by e-mail or other comparable modern electronic transmission presents a greater problem for the party seeking to rely upon such transmission as constituting due service. An e-mail communication which is available but not taken up or even one which is read from a screen with no hard copy taken, can hardly be said to have been delivered to the recipient or 'left at his proper address'. It should be remembered that the Agricultural

---

1   [2000] 04 EG 135.

Holdings Act 1986 ante-dated most of the modern, electronic forms of communication and Parliament could not have anticipated such a problem arising.

Section 36(2) and (3) of the Agricultural Tenancies Act 1995 specifically provides that in the case of farm business tenancies, text transmitted by 'facsimile or other electronic means' is not to constitute due service unless service in that way is authorised 'by written agreement made at any time before the giving of the Notice'. The application therefore of *Hastie and Jenkinson v McMahon*[1] to the service of notices under the Agricultural Holdings Act 1986, should not be relied upon as necessarily being applicable to 1986 Act cases.

1   [1991] 1 All ER 255.

SECTION 2

Statutes and statutory instruments

537 **Definitions**. Delete 'Sub-s (3) above' at end of para, and insert 's 49(3)'.

Insert the following statutory instruments:

DAIRY PRODUCE QUOTAS REGULATIONS 1997

SI 1997/733

The Minister of Agriculture, Fisheries and Food and the Secretary of State, being Ministers designated for the purposes of section 2(2) of the European Communities Act 1972 in relation to the common agricultural policy of the European Community, acting jointly, in exercise of the powers conferred on them by that section and of all other powers enabling them in that behalf, hereby make the following Regulations:

Title and commencement

1. These Regulations may be cited as the Dairy Produce Quotas Regulations 1997 and shall come into force on 1st April 1997.

Interpretation

2. (1) In these Regulations, unless the context otherwise requires—

'agricultural area' includes areas used for horticulture, fruit growing, seed growing, dairy farming and livestock breeding and keeping, areas of land used as grazing land, meadow land, osier land, market gardens and nursery grounds and areas of land used for woodlands where that use is ancillary to the farming of land for other agricultural purposes;

'authorised officer' means any person who is authorised by the Intervention Board, in writing, either generally or specifically, to act in matters arising under these Regulations or the Community legislation;

'the Commission Regulation' means Commission Regulation (EEC) No 536/93, laying down detailed rules on the application of the levy on milk and milk products, as last amended by Commission Regulation (EEC) No 470/94 and as corrected by the first corrigendum at OJ No L273, 16.11.95, p 54;

'the Community compensation scheme' means the scheme instituted by Council Regulation (EEC) No 2187/93 providing for an offer of compensation to certain producers of milk and milk products

temporarily prevented from carrying on their trade and
Commission Regulation (EEC) No 2648/93 laying down
detailed rules for the application of Council Regulation (EEC)
No 2187/93;

'the Community legislation' means the Commission Regulation, the
Council Regulation, Council Regulation 2055/93 and the legislation listed in Schedule 1;

'consent or sole interest notice' means a notice, in relation to a holding or part of a holding, provided by the person required under
these Regulations to provide the notice, and certifying—

    (a) either that he is the occupier of that holding or part of a
holding and that no other person has an interest in that holding or part of the holding, or

    (b) that all persons having an interest in the holding or part of
the holding the value of which interest might be reduced by
the apportionment or prospective apportionment to which
the notice relates agree to that apportionment or proposed
prospective apportionment;

'the Council Regulation' means Council Regulation (EEC) No
3950/92 establishing an additional levy in the milk and milk
products sector, as last amended by [Council Regulation (EC)
No 1256/1999];

'Council Regulation 2055/93' means Council Regulation (EEC) No
2055/93, allocating a special reference quantity to certain producers of milk and milk products;

'cow' includes a heifer that has calved;

'dairy enterprise' means an area stated by the occupier of that area to
be run as a self-contained dairy produce business;

'dairy produce' means the produce, expressed in kilograms or litres
of milk (one kilogram being 0.971 litres), in respect of which
levy is payable under the Community legislation;

'Dairy Produce Quota Tribunal' has the meaning assigned to it by
regulation 34;

'delivery' has the meaning assigned to it by Article 9(g) of the
Council Regulation (which sets out definitions) and 'deliver'
shall be construed accordingly;

'direct sale' means a sale which comes within Article 9(h) of the
Council Regulation;

'direct sales quota' means the quantity of dairy produce which may be
sold by direct sale from a holding in a quota year without the
direct seller in occupation of that holding being liable to pay levy;

'direct seller' means a person who produces milk and treats or
processes that milk into milk or milk products on his holding
and subsequently sells or transfers free of charge that milk or
those milk products without their having been treated or
processed by an undertaking which treats or processes milk or
milk products;

'eligible heifer' means any heifer, which, at the date of service of a notice referred to in regulation 14(2)(b)(i), was on land subject to the notice and calves for the first time on a day when the notice has effect, or which at the date of the coming into force of an order referred to in regulation 14(2)(b)(ii), was on land designated by the order and calves for the first time on a day when the order is in force;

'holding' has the meaning assigned to it by Article 9(d) of the Council Regulation;

'interest' includes the interest of a mortgage or heritable creditor and a trustee, but does not include the interest of a beneficiary under a trust or settlement or, in Scotland, the estate of a superior;

'Intervention Board' means the Intervention Board for Agricultural Produce established under section 6(1) of the European Communities Act 1972;

'levy' means the levy, payable under the Community legislation and these Regulations to the Intervention Board and described in Article 1 of the Council Regulation (which deals with the fixing of the levy);

'Minister', as regards anything in these Regulations relating to—

(a) England and Wales, means the Minister of Agriculture, Fisheries and Food and the Secretary of State for Wales acting jointly;

(b) Scotland, means the Secretary of State for Scotland;

(c) Northern Ireland, shall be construed in accordance with paragraph (3); and

(d) the United Kingdom, means the Ministers;

'Ministers' means all those to whom the definition of 'the Minister' relates, acting jointly;

'national reserve' means the reserve described in regulation 12, constituted so as to comply with Article 5 of the Council Regulation (which deals with confiscation and distribution of quota);

'occupier' includes, in relation to land in respect of which there is no occupier, the person entitled to grant occupation of that land to another person, and during the currency of an interest referred to in regulation 7(5)(a), the person entitled to grant occupation when that interest terminates, and 'occupation' shall be construed accordingly;

'producer' has the meaning assigned to it by Article 9(c) of the Council Regulation;

'prospective apportionment' in relation to quota on a holding means apportionment of quota under regulation 9 which will take place if there is a change of occupation of a part of the holding to which the prospective apportionment relates (other than a change to which regulation 7(5) applies) within six months of that prospective apportionment;

'purchaser' means a purchaser as defined in Article 9(e) of the Council Regulation and approved by the Intervention Board pursuant to Article 7(1)(a) of the Commission Regulation;

'purchaser quota' means the quantity of dairy produce which may be delivered by wholesale delivery to a purchaser during a quotas year without that purchaser being liable to pay levy;

'purchaser special quota' means the quantity of dairy produce which may be delivered by wholesale deliveries against producers' special quotas to a purchaser during a quota year without that purchaser being liable to pay levy;

'qualifying cow' means any eligible heifer which calves at a time when the number of eligible heifers exceeds the replacement number;

'qualifying day' means, in respect of any qualifying cow, the day it calves and each day or part of a day thereafter during which the notice referred to in regulation 14(2)(b)(i) has effect or during which the order referred to in regulation 14(2)(b)(ii) is in force;

'quota' means direct sales quota or wholesale quota, as the case may be;

'quota year' means any of the periods of 12 months described in Article 1 of the Council Regulation (which deals with the fixing of the levy);

'registered wholesale quota' means quota registered in accordance with regulation 24(2)(a);

'the 1984 Regulations' means the Dairy Produce Quotas Regulations 1984;

'replacement number' means the nearest integer to 20 per cent of the total number of dairy cows on the land subject to the notice referred to in regulation 14(2)(b)(i), or designated by the order referred to in regulation 14(2)(b)(ii), as at the date of service of the notice or (as the case may be) the coming into force of the order, and where 20 per cent of the total number is half way between two integers the nearest even integer shall be deemed to be the nearest integer;

'Scottish Islands area' means any one of—

(a) ...

(b) the islands of Orkney; or

(c) the islands of Islay, Jura, Gigha, Arran, Bute, Great Cumbrae and Little Cumbrae and the Kintyre peninsula south of Tarbert;

'special quota' means the quota referred to in Article 4(3) of the Council Regulation and in Article 1(1) of Council Regulation 2055/93;

'submit' means, in relation to a document submitted to the Intervention Board, the act of sending that document as evidenced by proof of posting or delivery to a courier service;

'total direct sales quota' means the total quantity of dairy produce which may be sold by direct sale from a holding in a quota year without the direct seller in occupation of that holding being liable to pay levy;

'total wholesale quota' means the total quantity of dairy produce which may be delivered by wholesale delivery from a holding in a quota year without the producer in occupation of that holding being liable to pay levy;

'transferee', means—

    (a) where quota is transferred with land, a person who replaces another person as occupier of that holding or part of a holding; and

    (b) in any other case, the transferee of quota;

'transferor', means—

    (a) where quota is transferred with land, a person who is replaced by another person as occupier of a holding or part of a holding; and

    (b) in any other case, the transferor of quota;

'unused quota' means quota remaining unused after any direct sales or wholesale deliveries have been taken into account, adjusted in accordance with Article 2(2) of the Commission Regulation (which deals with the fat content of milk), and 'used quota' shall be construed accordingly;

'wholesale delivery' means delivery from a producer to a purchaser;

'wholesale quota' means the quantity of dairy produce which may be delivered by wholesale delivery to a purchaser (to the extent specified in relation to that purchaser under these Regulations), from a holding in a quota year without the producer in occupation of that holding being liable to pay levy.

(2) In these Regulations, unless the context otherwise requires—

    (a) any reference to a numbered regulation or Schedule shall be construed as a reference to the regulation or Schedule so numbered in these Regulations;

    (b) any reference in a regulation or Schedule to a numbered paragraph shall be construed as a reference to the paragraph so numbered in that regulation or Schedule; and

    (c) any reference in a paragraph to a numbered or lettered sub-paragraph shall be construed as a reference to the sub-paragraph so numbered or lettered in that paragraph.

(3) In their application to Northern Ireland these Regulations shall have effect with the substitution, for references to the Minister, of references to the Department of Agriculture for Northern Ireland.

Notes

Amendments. Para (1): in definition 'the Council Regulation' words in square brackets substituted in relation to England by SI 2000/698, regs 2, 3(a), in relation to Scotland by SSI 2000/52, regs 2, 3(a), and in relation to Wales by SI 2000/972, regs 2, 3(a); in definition 'Scottish Islands area' para (a) revoked in relation to England by SI 2000/698, regs 2, 3(b), in relation to Scotland by SSI 2000/52, regs 2, 3(b), and in relation to Wales by SI 2000/972, regs 2, 3(b).

Transfer of Functions. Functions of the Minister, in respect of the functions exercisable by the Secretary of State for Wales, transferred to the National Assembly for Wales, by the National Assembly for Wales (Transfer of Functions) Order 1999, SI 1999/672, arts 2, 4, Sch 1.

Establishment of quota

3. Total direct sales quota and total wholesale quota for any person and purchaser quota for any purchaser in respect of any quota year shall be established in accordance with these Regulations and the Community legislation.

Determination of levy

4. For the purposes of Article 2(1) of the Council Regulation (which deals with the calculation of the levy), the contribution of producers who make wholesale deliveries towards the levy shall be established, in accordance with the provisions of that Article, at the level of the purchaser.

Milk equivalence of dairy produce

5. (1) For the purposes of Article 1(2) of the Commission Regulation (which deals with milk equivalence of dairy produce) the milk equivalence of dairy produce shall be calculated on the basis that each kilogram of dairy produce shall equal such quantity of milk referred to in paragraph (2) as is required to make that kilogram of dairy produce.

(2) The milk to which paragraph (1) relates is milk the fat content of which has not been altered since milking.

Adjustment of purchaser quota

6. (1) Where any wholesale quota is increased or reduced in accordance with the Community legislation or these Regulations, the purchaser quota of any purchaser to whom that quota is applicable shall be correspondingly increased or reduced.

(2) On any transaction to which the second sub-paragraph of Article 2(2) of the Council Regulation (which deals with replacements of purchasers and changes of purchasers by producers) applies, or on any permanent conversion of quota under regulation 16, any purchaser whose purchaser quota has been increased by virtue of such a transaction (other than as a result of a temporary transfer of quota under regulation 13) or such a conversion of quota shall submit to the Intervention Board—

(a) no later than [21st May 1997 or 28 days after the date on which the transaction or conversion of quota takes place (whichever is the later)], a statement setting out particulars of the transaction or conversion; and

(b) where appropriate, a declaration made and signed by the producer that the purchaser whose purchaser quota is to decrease has been notified of the particulars set out in the statement referred to in sub-paragraph (a).

(3) The statement referred to in paragraph (2)(a) and the declaration referred to in paragraph (2)(b) shall be made in such form as may reasonably be required by the Intervention Board.

(4) Where during a quota year a producer changes from being registered with a purchaser to being registered with any other purchaser—

    (a) for the purposes of calculation of levy liability under regulation 18 in that quota year, any purchaser with whom he is newly registered shall have his purchaser quota increased by an amount equivalent to such part of that producer's registered wholesale quota as that producer shall determine;

    (b) the amount of the increase of purchaser quota determined in accordance with sub-paragraph (a) shall not include the amount of quota necessary to cover the deliveries made by the producer before the date of the change of purchaser, adjusted if necessary in accordance with the second sub-paragraph of Article 2(2) of the Commission Regulation, and such amount of quota shall remain available to the original purchaser; and

    (c) at the beginning of the quota year following the quota year referred to in sub-paragraph (a), the purchaser with whom the producer is newly registered shall have his purchaser quota increased by such part of the producer's remaining registered wholesale quota as that producer shall determine;

and corresponding reductions of the purchaser quota of the original purchaser shall be made and where there are adjustments of quota of a producer registered with more than one purchaser, similar adjustments of purchaser quota shall be made.

(5) Where the amount of wholesale quota available to a producer changes as a result of a transfer of quota under regulation 7, 11 or 13, or as a result of a conversion of quota under regulation 16, that producer shall notify each purchaser with whom his wholesale quota is registered within seven working days of the change.

Notes

    Amendment. Para (2): in sub-para (a) words in square brackets substituted by SI 1997/1093, reg 2(2).

Transfer of quota with transfer of land

7. (1) For the purposes of Article 7 of the Council Regulation (which deals with transfer of quota with a holding when the holding is sold, leased, transferred by inheritance or subjected to other cases of transfer involving comparable legal effects for producers), on a transfer of any holding or part of a holding, other than a transfer of a kind to which paragraph (5) or (7) refers, the transferee shall submit to the Intervention Board—

    [(a) a notice of transfer in such form as may reasonably be required by the Intervention Board—

    (i)   in the case of a transfer made by lease before 1st March, on or before 1st March in the quota year in which the transfer takes place;

    (ii) in the case of a transfer made otherwise than by lease, on or before 31st March in the quota year in which the transfer takes place;

and in any case not later than 28 days after the change of occupation of the holding, or part of the holding; and]

  (b) such other information relating to the transfer, and within such time, as the Intervention Board may reasonably require.

(2) The notice referred to in paragraph (1)(a) shall, in the case of a transfer of part of a holding, include—

  (a) a statement, signed by the transferor and transferee, that they have agreed that the quota shall be apportioned taking account of the areas used for milk production as specified in the statement or to the effect that no such apportionment has been agreed; and

  (b) where such an apportionment has been agreed, a consent or sole interest notice, provided by the transferor in respect of the entirety of the holding.

(3) Where there is a transfer of part of a holding—

  (a) an apportionment of the quota relating to the holding shall be carried out in accordance with regulation 8; and

  (b) any dairy produce which has been sold by direct sale or delivered by wholesale delivery from the holding during the quota year in which the change of occupation takes place and prior to that transfer shall be deemed, for the purposes of any levy calculation, to have been sold or delivered from each part of the holding in proportion to that apportionment, unless the parties agree otherwise and notify the Intervention Board of the agreement in such a form as the Intervention Board may reasonably require, no later than 28 days after the change of occupation, and in any event no later than 7 working days after the end of the quota year in which the transfer takes place.

(4) A prospective apportionment of quota in respect of a part of a holding may be made in accordance with regulation 9.

(5) No person shall transfer quota on a transfer of any holding or part of a holding in the following cases—

  (a) the grant of:

    (i)   a licence to occupy land;

    (ii) the tenancy of any land under which a holding, or part of a holding, in England and Wales is occupied for a period of less than ten months;

      (iii) the lease of any land under which a holding, or part of a holding, in Scotland is occupied for a period of less than eight months;

      (iv) the tenancy of any land under which a holding, or part of a holding, in Northern Ireland is occupied for a period of less than twelve months;

    (b) the termination of a licence, tenancy or lease to which sub-paragraph (a) applies.

(6) [Where a notice of transfer in the form required by the Intervention Board has not been submitted (in the case of a transfer made by lease) on or before 1st March or (in the case of a transfer made otherwise than by lease) on or before 31st March in the quota year in which the transfer takes place,] then for the purposes of any levy calculation—

    (a) the unused quota transferred with such transfer shall not be treated as a part of the transferee's quota entitlement for the quota year in which the transfer takes effect but shall be treated as if it remained unused quota available where appropriate for reallocation by the Intervention Board in that quota year in accordance with paragraph 7 of Schedule 5;

    (b) the notice shall be disregarded by the Intervention Board for the quota year to which it applies and shall not be noted on any register maintained under regulation 24 until the following quota year; and

    (c) a transferee shall not be entitled to demand that, by reason of such a transfer, an amendment be made to the amount of quota, if any, which has been reallocated to him under Schedule 5 for the quota year in which the transfer takes effect.

(7) No person shall transfer quota on a transfer of a holding or part of a holding where the transfer would result in an increase or reduction in the total direct sales quota or total wholesale quota available for use by dairy enterprises located within a Scottish Islands area.

Notes

   Amendments. Para (1): sub-para (a) substituted in relation to England by SI 2000/698, regs 2, 4(a), in relation to Scotland by SSI 2000/52, regs 2, 4(a), and in relation to Wales by SI 2000/972, regs 2, 4(a).

   Para (6): words in square brackets substituted in relation to England by SI 2000/698, regs 2, 4(b), in relation to Scotland by SSI 2000/52, regs 2, 4(b), and in relation to Wales by SI 2000/972, regs 2, 4(b).

Apportionment of quota

   8. Subject to regulations 7(5) and (7), 9(4) and (5) and 10, where there is a transfer of part of a holding, the apportionment of the quota or special quota, relating to that holding, shall be carried out—

    (a) in accordance with the agreed apportionment set out in the notice referred to in regulation 7(1)(a); or

(b) where there is no such agreement—
    (i) in England and Wales and Northern Ireland, by arbitration in accordance with Schedules 2 and 4 respectively;
    (ii) in Scotland, in accordance with Schedule 3.

Prospective apportionment of quota

9. (1) The occupier of a holding who intends that a prospective apportionment of quota will be applied to it shall submit to the Intervention Board an application in such a form as may reasonably be required for this purpose by the Intervention Board, requesting either—

(a) that a prospective apportionment of quota relating to the holding be made taking account of areas used for milk production as set out in the application; or

(b) that a prospective apportionment of quota be ascertained by arbitration in accordance with Schedule 2 in England and Wales and with Schedule 4 in Northern Ireland, or in Scotland in accordance with Schedule 3.

(2) A request for a prospective apportionment of quota may be revoked by a notice in writing to the Intervention Board, signed by the occupier of the holding to which the prospective apportionment relates.

(3) Where the occupier of a holding requests that a prospective apportionment be made in accordance with paragraph (1)(a), or gives notice in writing of the revocation of such a request, that request or notice shall be accompanied by a consent or sole interest notice in respect of the entirety of the holding.

(4) Where there is a change of occupation of part of a holding (other than a change to which regulation 7(5) applies) and within the six months preceding that change of occupation—

(a) the occupier of that holding has requested a prospective apportionment of quota in respect of that part of the holding and has submitted a notice in accordance with regulation 7(1), indicating that an apportionment of quota has been agreed; or

(b) a prospective apportionment of quota relating to that part of that holding has been or is in the process of being made by virtue of Schedule 2, 3 or 4,

the apportionment of quota shall be carried out in accordance with paragraph (5).

(5) Where quota is apportioned in accordance with this paragraph, the apportionment shall be carried out in accordance with—

(a) any prospective apportionment of quota relating to that part of that holding made under paragraph (1) unless the request for that prospective apportionment was revoked before the change of occupation to which it relates takes place;

(b) if no such prospective apportionment has been made, any prospective apportionment which is in the process of being made under paragraph (1); and

(c) in any other case, regulation 8.

Notification by the Intervention Board of apportionment of quota by arbitration

10. (1) Where the Intervention Board has reasonable grounds for believing—

(a) that the areas used for milk production on a holding are not as specified in a notice or application submitted for the purposes of regulation 7 or 9(1) respectively; or

(b) that the areas used for milk production on a holding were not as agreed between the parties at the time of apportionment in a case where no notice or application has yet been submitted for the purposes of the aforementioned regulations,

it may give notice of this fact to the person who submitted the form, or in a case where no such notice or application was made, to the transferee.

(2) In any case to which paragraph (1) applies the apportionment or prospective apportionment of that quota shall be made—

(a) in England and Wales and Northern Ireland by arbitration in accordance with Schedules 2 and 4 respectively;

(b) in Scotland in accordance with Schedule 3.

Transfer of quota without transfer of land

11. (1) For the purposes of [sub-paragraph (e)] of Article 8 of the Council Regulation (which permits the authorisation of a transfer of quota without transfer of the corresponding land, with the aim of improving the structure of milk production at the level of the holding), an application for transfer of quota without transfer of land, other than an application for transfer of a kind to which paragraph (9) below refers, shall be submitted by the transferee to the Intervention Board for approval no later than [8th May 1997 or ten working days before the intended date of the transfer (whichever is the later)] and that application shall be in such form as may be reasonably required for that purpose by the Intervention Board.

(2) The application referred to in paragraph (1) shall include—

(a) a statement, signed by the transferor and transferee, that they have agreed to the transfer of quota and explaining how the transfer is necessary to improve the structure of the business of the transferor and transferee;

(b) a consent or sole interest notice signed by the transferor in respect of the entirety of the holding from which the quota is to be transferred;

   (c) an undertaking by the transferor that he—
- (i) has not transferred quota onto his holding in accordance with the provisions of this regulation other than by a transfer in respect of which, pursuant to paragraph (7), he has been released from the undertaking referred to in sub-paragraph (d)(i) in the course of the quota year in which the application is made, or in the preceding quota year;
- (ii) will not transfer quota onto his holding under regulations 7, 11 or 13 in the period between the date of submission of the application and the end of the quota year following the quota year in which the transfer without land takes place; and
- (iii) will not, through his connection with or involvement in another business, seek to circumvent the restrictions at paragraphs (i) and (ii) above; and

   (d) an undertaking by the transferee that he—
- (i) will not transfer quota from his holding under regulation 7, 11 or 13 in the period between the date of submission of the application and the end of the quota year following the quota year in which the transfer without land takes place;
- (ii) will not, through his connection with or involvement in another business, seek to circumvent the restriction at paragraph (i) above.

(3) The reference to the transfer of quota in sub-paragraphs (c)(ii) and (d)(i) of paragraph (2) shall include temporary transfer under regulation 13 but exclude transfer on inheritance.

(4) Where it has received an application under paragraph (1), the Intervention Board may require that the transferor or transferee shall produce such other information relating to the application, and within such time, as the Intervention Board reasonably may determine.

(5) Where the Intervention Board approves an application under paragraph (1), the transferee shall, no later than 28 days after the transfer takes place, and in any event [not after 31st March in] the quota year in which the transfer takes place, submit to the Intervention Board, in such form as the Intervention Board may reasonably require, a statement of the amounts of used and unused quota available to the transferor and transferee on the date of the transfer.

(6) Where a transferee fails to submit a statement in accordance with the requirements of paragraph (5), the Intervention Board shall revoke its approval.

(7) Where an application to transfer quota without transfer of land has been approved by the Intervention Board, and the statement required by paragraph (5) has been submitted in accordance with that paragraph, the Intervention Board may release a transferee from the undertaking referred to in paragraph (2)(d)(i), where the Intervention Board is satisfied that exceptional circumstances, resulting in a significant fall in milk production which could not have been avoided or foreseen by the transferee at the time of the submission of the application under paragraph (1), justify that release.

(8) The exceptional circumstances referred to in paragraph (7) are—

(a) the inability of the transferee to conduct his business over a pro-longed period as a result of the onset of ill-health, injury or disability;

(b) a natural disaster seriously affecting the holding;

(c) the accidental destruction of buildings used for the purposes of milk production;

(d) without prejudice to sub-paragraph (e), an outbreak of illness or disease seriously affecting the dairy herd;

(e) the serving of a notice or the making of a declaration under an order made under section 17 of the Animal Health Act 1981 (in respect of places or areas in Great Britain) or the making of a declaration under an order made under article 12(1) of the Diseases of Animals (Northern Ireland) Order 1981 (in respect of places or areas in Northern Ireland) or the adoption of an emergency order under section 1 of the Food and Environment Protection Act 1985;

(f) the loss of a significant proportion of the forage area as a result of the compulsory purchase of the holding or part of the holding;

(g) where the transferee is a tenant, the serving of an incontestable notice to quit under the provisions of section 26 of and Schedule 3 to the Agricultural Holdings Act 1986 dealing with the serving of incontestable notices to quit where the tenant is not at fault; and

(h) in the quota year commencing 1st April 1997, the slaughter of animals forming part of the dairy herd pursuant to the powers conferred upon the Minister under section 32(1)(b) of the Animal Health Act 1981, as animals having been exposed to the infection of bovine spongiform encephalopathy.

(9) As provided for in the fourth indent of the first paragraph of Article 8 of the Council Regulation (which provides for the determination of regions within which such transfers may be authorised), no applications for a transfer of quota may be submitted pursuant to paragraph (1) where the transfer would result in an increase or reduction in the total direct sales quota or total wholesale quota available for use by dairy enterprises located within a Scottish Islands area.

Notes

Amendments. Para (1): first words in square brackets substituted in relation to England by SI 2000/698, regs 2, 5(a), in relation to Scotland by SSI 2000/52, regs 2, 5(a), and in relation to Wales by SI 2000/972, regs 2, 5(a); second words in square brackets substituted by SI 1997/1093, reg 2(3).

Para (5): words in square brackets substituted in relation to England by SI 2000/698, regs 2, 5(b), in relation to Scotland by SSI 2000/52, regs 2, 5(b), and in relation to Wales by SI 2000/972, regs 2, 5(b).

Transfer of Functions. Functions of the Minister, in respect of the functions exercisable by the Secretary of State for Wales, transferred to the National Assembly for Wales, by the National Assembly for Wales (Transfer of Functions) Order 1999, SI 1999/672, arts 2, 4, Sch 1.

National reserve

12. (1) The national reserve shall comprise such wholesale and direct sales quota as is not for the time being allocated to any person, including any quota withdrawn under these Regulations.

(2) The Minister may make allocations from the national reserve in accordance with the Community legislation and these Regulations.

Notes

Transfer of Functions. Functions of the Minister, in respect of the functions exercisable by the Secretary of State for Wales, transferred to the National Assembly for Wales, by the National Assembly for Wales (Transfer of Functions) Order 1999, SI 1999/672, arts 2, 4, Sch 1.

Temporary transfer of quota

13. (1) For the purposes of Article 6 of the Council Regulation (which deals with the temporary transfer of quota), . . . a producer may agree with any other producer to make a temporary transfer, other than a temporary transfer of a kind to which paragraph (4) below refers, of all or part of any unused quota which is registered under regulation 24 as permanently held by him for a period of one quota year to that other producer.

(2) The Intervention Board may require a reasonable charge to be paid for the registration of any temporary transfer of a quota, but only if the transfer takes place within a quota year in respect of which it has announced before the beginning of that quota year that it intends to make such a charge, in such a manner as it considered likely to come to the attention of producers.

(3) Where there is an agreement to make a temporary transfer of quota under paragraph (1), the transferee shall notify the Intervention Board of the agreement in such form as may reasonably be required by the Intervention Board, and shall submit the notice, accompanied by any charge payable under paragraph (2), to the Intervention Board no later than 31st [March] in the quota year in which the agreement is made.

(4) No producer shall agree with any other producer to make a temporary transfer of quota which would result in a reduction in the total direct sales quota or total wholesale quota available for use by dairy enterprises located within a Scottish Islands area.

(5) . . .

Notes

Amendments. Para (1): words omitted revoked in relation to England by SI 2000/698, regs 2, 6(a), in relation to Scotland by SSI 2000/52, regs 2, 6(a), and in relation to Wales by SI 2000/972, regs 2, 6(a).

Para (3): word in square brackets substituted in relation to England by SI 2000/698, regs 2, 6(b), in relation to Scotland by SSI 2000/52, regs 2, 6(b), and in relation to Wales by SI 2000/972, regs 2, 6(b).

Para (5): revoked in relation to England by SI 2000/698, regs 2, 6(c), in relation to Scotland by SSI 2000/52, regs 2, 6(c), and in relation to Wales by SI 2000/972, regs 2, 6(c).

Temporary reallocation of quota

14. (1) For the purposes of Article 2(4) of the Council Regulation and Article 5 of the Commission Regulation (which together deal with the reallocation of excess levy), the Intervention Board may, for any quota year, award to a producer referred to in paragraph (2) a temporary reallocation of an amount of any surplus quota corresponding to a proportion of any levy collected in excess of the levy actually due in that year, in accordance with the provisions of this regulation.

(2) This regulation shall apply to—

(a) a producer who is affected by a formal acknowledgement of an error in the levy calculation, made pursuant to Article 5(1)(a) of the Commission Regulation; and

(b) a producer who has quota registered as his in relation to a holding which—

(i) is in whole or in part subject to a notice prohibiting or regulating the movement of dairy cows pursuant to an order made under the Animal Health Act 1981 or the Diseases of Animals (Northern Ireland) Order 1981, or

(ii) is situated wholly or partly within an area which at any time during that quota year has been designated by an emergency order under section 1 of the Food and Environment Protection Act 1985.

(3) Subject to paragraphs (4) and (5), a producer referred to in paragraph (2)(b) may be awarded a temporary reallocation of surplus quota for any quota year in which the notice referred to in paragraph (2)(b)(i) or (as the case may be) the order referred to in paragraph (2)(b)(ii) has effect, and the amount of any such award shall be calculated either—

(a) as the amount equal to 16 litres per qualifying cow per qualifying day in any quota year; or

(b) as the amount by which in the quota year in question the producer's production exceeds his quota entitlement,

whichever amount is less.

(4) Where the notice referred to in paragraph (2)(b)(i) continues in effect or the order referred to in paragraph (2)(b)(ii) remains in force for a period beyond the quota year in respect of which a producer has received an award under paragraph (3), any award under that paragraph for the following quota year shall be calculated as if the number of the producer's qualifying cows were equal to that of his eligible heifers which calved during that period or (if the period extends beyond that following quota year) during that following quota year, notwithstanding the fact that when any such heifers calved the number of eligible heifers did not exceed the replacement number.

(5) An award under paragraph (3) above shall not be available in the same quota year to a producer who transfers unused quota under regulation 7 or 11, makes a temporary transfer of quota under regulation 13, or purchases cows or in-calf heifers for dairy purposes, unless the Intervention Board is satisfied that the agreement to transfer, temporarily transfer or purchase, was entered into before service of the notice to which paragraph (2)(b)(i) refers, or (as the case may be) before the coming into force of the order to which paragraph (2)(b)(ii) refers.

42

(6) A producer referred to in paragraph (2)(a) above may be awarded a temporary reallocation of surplus quota, for any quota year in respect of which the formal acknowledgement referred to in the Commission Regulation applies, which wholly or partially offsets the error in levy calculation to which the acknowledgement relates.

(7) In awarding a temporary reallocation of surplus quota for the purpose of this regulation the Intervention Board shall give priority to the producers referred to in paragraph (2)(a).

Special allocation of quota

15. Where, by reason of a mistake made by the Minister or any person acting on his behalf, a person has not been allocated any quota or has been allocated a smaller quantity of any such quota than he would have been allocated if the mistake had not been made, the Minister may allocate to that person such quota as will compensate, in whole or in part, for that mistake from the national reserve.

Notes

Transfer of Functions. Functions of the Minister, in respect of the functions exercisable by the Secretary of State for Wales, transferred to the National Assembly for Wales, by the National Assembly for Wales (Transfer of Functions) Order 1999, SI 1999/672, arts 2, 4, Sch 1.

Conversion of quota

16. (1) For the purposes of the provisions of Article 4(2) of the Council Regulation (which deals with changes from direct sales to wholesale delivery and vice versa), the second sub-paragraph of Article 2(2) of the Council Regulation (which deals with replacements of purchasers) and this regulation, a producer may apply to convert, temporarily or permanently, direct sales quota for wholesale quota or wholesale quota for direct sales quota.

(2) Where a producer wishes to convert quota permanently or temporarily in any quota year, he shall submit to the Intervention Board an application in such a form as the Intervention Board may reasonably require for that purpose and such application shall—

    (a) state the amount (if any) of the producer's direct sales quota, wholesale quota, direct sales and wholesale deliveries for the quota year in which the application is made, and the amount of unused quota which he holds at the time of the application and which he wishes the Intervention Board to convert; and

    (b) include such other information as the Intervention Board may reasonably require in order to assess whether the requirements of Article 4(2) of the Council Regulation and Article 2 of the Commission Regulation are fulfilled.

(3) The application referred to in paragraph (2) above shall be submitted by the producer to the Intervention Board by—

(a) 31st December in any year in the case of permanent conversion of quota; or

(b) 14th May in any year following the end of the quota year in which the temporary conversion of quota takes place, in the case of temporary conversion of quota.

(4) Subject to paragraph (5), where a producer has permanently converted quota in any quota year, he shall not subsequently in that quota year transfer out quota, of the type to which he has converted, whether temporarily or otherwise.

(5) In the quota year commencing 1st April 1997, where the Minister in accordance with section 32(1)(b) of the Animal Health Act 1981 has caused animals forming part of a producer's dairy herd, to be slaughtered as having been exposed to the infection of bovine spongiform encephalopathy, paragraph (4) above shall not apply to that producer.

Notes
    Transfer of Functions. Functions of the Minister, in respect of the functions exercisable by the Secretary of State for Wales, transferred to the National Assembly for Wales, by the National Assembly for Wales (Transfer of Functions) Order 1999, SI 1999/672, arts 2, 4, Sch 1.

Representative fat content of milk

17. A producer who in any quota year comes within the first indent of Article 2(1)(e) of the Commission Regulation (which deals with the representative fat content of milk from certain new producers) may benefit from the negative correction provided for in the second indent of Article 2(2) thereof only if, before 1st March in that quota year, he confirms to the Intervention Board that in that quota year he has maintained in his dairy herd breeds of cow with characteristics similar to those in the herd in the first twelve months of production and undertakes to maintain such breeds in his dairy herd for the remainder of that quota year.

Reallocation of quota and calculation of levy liability

18. Schedule 5 shall apply in respect of the reallocation of quota and the calculation of levy liability for the purposes of Article 2(1) of the Council Regulation (which deals with the calculation of the levy).

Prevention of avoidance of levy

19. (1) Subject to paragraph (2), where in any quota year a producer makes sales or deliveries of milk or milk products from milk produced by any cows and subsequently in the same quota year another producer makes sales or deliveries of milk or milk products from milk produced by any or all of the same cows, the second producer shall be deemed for the purposes of these Regulations to have made those sales or deliveries in the capacity of agent for the first producer.

(2) Paragraph (1) shall not apply where—

(a) an agreement has been entered into by the first producer for the sale or lease of the cows in question or the second producer has inherited them from the first producer; and

(b) the cows are kept on the second producer's holding.

Payment of levy

20. (1) For the purposes of Article 2(3) of the Council Regulation and Article 4 of the Commission Regulation (both of which deal with payment of levy by direct sellers), or Article 2(2) of the Council Regulation and Article 3 of the Commission Regulation (both of which deal with payment of levy by purchasers in respect of wholesale deliveries), levy shall be paid to the Intervention Board.

(2) Where any part of the levy remains unpaid after 1st September in any year, the Intervention Board may recover from the direct seller or (as the case may be) the purchaser, the amount of the levy outstanding at that date together with interest in respect of each day thereafter until the said amount is recovered at the rate of one percentage point above the sterling three month London interbank offered rate.

(3) For the purposes of the third sub-paragraph of Article 2(2) of the Council Regulation (which deals with deduction of levy liability), where a producer making wholesale deliveries to a purchaser exceeds his wholesale quota, following adjustment of that quota where appropriate and in accordance with Article 2(2) of the Commission Regulation, that purchaser may immediately deduct an amount corresponding to the amount of levy potentially payable by him in respect of the excess from the sums owed to the producer in respect of the deliveries.

Functions of the Intervention Board

21. The Intervention Board shall be the competent body for the purposes of Article 2(3) of the Council Regulation (which deals with payment of levy by direct sellers), and the competent authority for the purposes of Articles 1, 3, 4 and 7 of the Commission Regulation (which together deal with matters relating to the assessment of levy and the payment of levy by direct sellers and purchasers).

Annual statements

22. (1) The Intervention Board may, in respect of—

(a) any person in whose name any direct sales quota is registered and who fails to submit to the Intervention Board by 14th May in any year any declaration which he is required to forward by Article 4(2) of the Commission Regulation, or

(b) any purchaser approved by the Intervention Board in accordance with Article 7 of the Commission Regulation and who fails to submit to the Intervention Board by 14th May in any year any summary which he is required to forward by Article 3(2) of the Commission Regulation,

recover a reasonable charge in respect of any visit to any premises which the Intervention Board has reasonably considered that it should make in order to obtain the declaration or summary in question.

Disapplication of enactments

23. Nothing in section 47(2) of the Agricultural Marketing Act 1958 or Article 29 of the Agricultural Marketing (Northern Ireland) Order 1982 (which restrict the disclosure of certain information obtained under those enactments) shall restrict or apply to the disclosure of any information if, and in so far as, the disclosure is required or authorised by these Regulations or the Community legislation.

Registers to be prepared and maintained by the Intervention Board

24. (1) The Intervention Board shall—

    (a) prepare a direct sales register entry in respect of each direct seller setting out in particular—
        (i) his name;
        (ii) his trading address;
        (iii) a reference number which serves to identify the direct seller;
        (iv) the direct sales quota available to him for the quota year excluding the quota referred to in paragraph (v) below; and
        (v) quota issued to him as special quota,
        and shall send each direct seller a copy of the entry relating to him; and
    (b) maintain—
        (i) a direct sales register (being a register of entries referred to in sub-paragraph (1)(a)), and
        (ii) a register of particulars of direct sales by each direct seller.

(2) The Intervention Board shall—

    (a) prepare a wholesale register entry in respect of each producer setting out in particular—
        (i) his name;
        (ii) his trading address;
        (iii) a reference number which serves to identify the producer;
        (iv) the wholesale quota available to him for the quota year excluding the quota referred to in sub-paragraph (v);
        (v) quota issued to him as special quota; and
        (vi) a list of the names and addresses of each purchaser whose purchaser quota will be calculated to take into account all or part of that producer's total wholesale quota, and of the wholesale quota registered with each purchaser, showing the representative fat content base of that quota calculated in accordance with Article 2 of the Commission Regulation, and shall send to each producer a copy of the entry relating to him and to each purchaser named on the list referred to in

paragraph (vi) above a copy of that part of the entry relating to his purchaser quota; and
   (b) maintain a wholesale register (being a register of entries referred to in sub-paragraph (a)).

(3) The Intervention Board shall—

   (a) prepare a purchaser notice in respect of each purchaser setting out—
       (i)   his name,
       (ii) his purchaser quota,
       (iii) his purchaser special quota,

       and shall send each purchaser a copy of the notice relating to him; and
   (b) maintain a register of purchaser notices.

(4) For the purposes of paragraphs (1) and (2) above, where a holding comprises more than one dairy enterprise, a direct seller or a producer may, on presenting to the Intervention Board a consent or sole interest notice in respect of that holding, agree with the Intervention Board the partition of that holding between separate direct sales register entries or wholesale register entries as specified in the agreement.

(5) The Intervention Board may make such enquiries as it reasonably considers to be necessary for the purposes of ensuring the accuracy of the registers which it is required to maintain pursuant to this regulation and shall amend such registers—

   (a) to record any allocations or adjustments made under or by virtue of these Regulations, or
   (b) to make any correction or amendment which it reasonably considers to be necessary,

and where it makes a correction or amendment, it shall notify any person affected by that correction or amendment.

(6) In this regulation 'direct seller' and 'producer' include a person who occupies land with quota whether or not that person is engaged in the sale or delivery of dairy produce.

Inspection of entries in the Intervention Board's registers

25. The Intervention Board may, in response to a request in writing regarding a quota register entry referred to in regulation 24(1) or (2)—

   (a) by any person who is the direct seller or producer identified in that entry, or who gives the Intervention Board a statement in writing that he has an interest in the holding of the producer or direct seller identified in that entry; or
   (b) by a purchaser in relation to a specific purchaser in the register referred to in regulation 24(3)(b),

on payment of a reasonable charge, supply to such a person a copy of that quota register entry.

Obligations of direct sellers and purchasers with respect to registration and deliveries

26. (1) Each direct seller shall register his quota with the Intervention Board.

(2) Each producer (as defined in regulation 24(6)) who holds registered wholesale quota (including any producer who has temporarily ceased or who intends temporarily to cease making wholesale deliveries) shall register his quota with a purchaser and, if making deliveries, shall deliver to a purchaser.

(3) Each purchaser shall maintain, in respect of all producers whose register entries include that purchaser's name on the list referred to in regulation 24(2)(a)(vi)—

(a) a register as indicated in regulation 24(2)(b) in respect of that part of his purchaser quota attributable to each of those producers;

(b) a register of particulars of wholesale deliveries from each of those producers to that purchaser;

(c) the information required by Article 7 of the Commission Regulation (which deals with the records required in connection with levy assessment); and

(d) a system approved by the Intervention Board for sampling the milk of each producer and determining its fat content.

(4) Each purchaser shall amend the register referred to in paragraph (3)(a) on each occasion when, under these Regulations, the equivalent register maintained by the Intervention Board is required to be amended in relation to producers registered in that purchaser's register.

(5) Each purchaser shall register with the Intervention Board and shall—

(a) give an undertaking to the Intervention Board to abide by the provisions of these Regulations and the Community legislation and comply with that undertaking;

(b) inform the Intervention Board of any factor or change in circumstance which affect that purchaser's registration or its ability to comply with the undertaking referred to in sub-paragraph (a);

(c) confirm to each producer supplying that purchaser that the purchaser is registered and supply on request details of that registration; and

(d) notify each producer supplying that purchaser if that registration is rescinded.

Registers as evidence

27. Any entry in a register or notice required by these Regulations to be maintained by the Intervention Board shall in any proceedings be evidence of the matters stated therein.

Information

28. (1) Each purchaser or producer shall provide such information to the Intervention Board as the Intervention Board may reasonably require in order to perform its functions under these Regulations and the Community legislation.

(2) Each purchaser shall submit to the Intervention Board on request, in a form from time to time to be determined by the Intervention Board, such statistics and forecasts relating to deliveries made or to be made to him, as reasonably may be required by the Intervention Board for the purpose of monitoring deliveries in relation to the total quantity for the United Kingdom referred to in Article 3(2) of the Council Regulation, and any such statistics shall be submitted within three working days of the end of the period to which the statistics relate, and any such forecast shall be submitted within 28 days of receipt by the purchaser of the request to provide such forecast.

(3) The Intervention Board shall copy such records to each purchaser as that purchaser reasonably may require for the purposes of his registration obligations under these Regulations and Article 3 of the Commission Regulation (which deals with the assessment and payment of levy).

Access to relevant information

28A. [(1) The Intervention Board may, upon receiving an appropriate request by the Minister, allow the Minister access to relevant information.

(2) For the purposes of paragraph (1) above—

  (a) an 'appropriate request' is one expressed to be for the purpose of enabling the Minister to—
    (i) determine from whom any charge payable under regulation 4(2)(g) of the Charges for Inspections and Controls Regulations 1997 is recoverable; or
    (ii) calculate any charge payable under those Regulations which relates to raw milk; and
  (b) 'access to relevant information' means—
    (i) inspection of—
      (aa) the entries in the registers which are referred to in regulation 24 of these Regulations; and
      (bb) such information as is received by the Intervention Board pursuant to regulation 28(2) of these Regulations; and
    (ii) the provision of a copy of any of those entries or such information, as appropriate.]

Notes

  Transfer of Functions. Functions of the Minister, in respect of the functions exercisable by the Secretary of State for Wales, transferred to the National Assembly for Wales, by the National Assembly for Wales (Transfer of Functions) Order 1999, SI 1999/672, arts 2, 4, Sch 1.

Withholding or recovery of compensation

29. Where a producer has submitted an application for compensation in accordance with the Community compensation scheme and it appears to the Minister that the producer has made a false or misleading statement in his application or has failed to comply with any of the requirements of that scheme, the Minister may withhold or recover on demand from that producer the whole or any part of the compensation payable or paid to him.

Notes

Transfer of Functions. Functions of the Minister, in respect of the functions exercisable by the Secretary of State for Wales, transferred to the National Assembly for Wales, by the National Assembly for Wales (Transfer of Functions) Order 1999, SI 1999/672, arts 2, 4, Sch 1.

Powers of authorised officers

30. (1) An authorised officer may, at all reasonable hours and on producing some duly authenticated document showing his authority, exercise the powers specified in this regulation for the purposes of ascertaining whether an offence under regulation 31(1)(a), (b) or (c) has been or is being committed.

(2) For the purposes of this regulation, an authorised officer may enter upon a holding [or any other premises of a relevant person].

(3) An authorised officer who has entered upon a holding [or any other premises of a relevant person] by virtue of this regulation may—

(a) inspect any land (other than land used only as a dwelling) and any record or document, including any document kept by means of a computer, which relates to the allocation or transfer of quota or the trade in, or production of milk or milk products;

(b) seize and retain any such record or document which he has reason to believe may be required as evidence in proceedings under regulation 31(1)(a), (b) or (c).

(4) A [relevant person] shall render all reasonable assistance to the authorised officer in relation to the matters mentioned in paragraph (1) above and in particular shall produce any such record or document and supply such additional information relating to the allocation to him of quota, the transfer to or from him of quota and the trade in or production of milk or milk products, as the authorised officer may reasonably require.

(5) In the case of a record or document kept by means of a computer a [relevant person] shall, if so required, provide any such record or document in a form in which it may be taken away.

[(6) In this regulation, a 'relevant person' means a producer, a purchaser, any employee or agent of a producer or of a purchaser, any milk haulier, or any person undertaking butterfat testing for purchasers in a laboratory.]

Notes

Amendments. Para (2): words in square brackets inserted in relation to England by SI 2000/698, regs 2, 7(a), in relation to Scotland by SSI 2000/52, regs 2, 7(a), and in relation to Wales by SI 2000/972, regs 2, 7(a).

Para (3): words in square brackets inserted in relation to England by SI 2000/698, regs 2, 7(a), in relation to Scotland by SSI 2000/52, regs 2, 7(a), and in relation to Wales by SI 2000/972, regs 2, 7(a).

Paras (4) and (5): words in square brackets substituted in relation to England by SI 2000/698, regs 2, 7(b), in relation to Scotland by SSI 2000/52, regs 2, 7(b), and in relation to Wales by SI 2000/972, regs 2, 7(b).

Para (6): inserted in relation to England by SI 2000/698, regs 2, 7(c), in relation to Scotland by SSI 2000/52, regs 2, 7(c), and in relation to Wales by SI 2000/972, reg 2, 7(c).

Penalties

31. (1) Any person who—

(a) fails without reasonable excuse to comply with a requirement imposed on him by or under these Regulations or the Community legislation, or

(b) in connection with these Regulations or the Community legislation, makes a statement or uses a document which he knows to be false in a material particular or recklessly makes a statement or uses a document which is false in a material particular; or

(c) disposes of quota which he knows or might reasonably be expected to know is incorrectly registered in his name,

shall be guilty of an offence and liable, on summary conviction, to a fine not exceeding level 5 on the standard scale or, on conviction on indictment, to a fine.

(2) The Minister may, following any conviction under paragraph (1)(b) against which there is no successful appeal, by notice served (within the period of 12 months following the date specified in paragraph (3)) on the person to whose quota that conviction relates withdraw his quota to such extent as may reasonably be regarded by the Minister as being attributable to the falsehood on which the conviction was founded.

(3) The date referred to in paragraph (2) above is—

(a) in the case of a conviction against which there is no appeal, the date on which the right to appeal against that conviction expires; and

(b) in the case of a conviction against which there is an unsuccessful appeal—

(i) if there is no right of appeal against the result of that unsuccessful appeal, the date of that result; and

(ii) if there is a right of appeal against that result but no appeal is made, the date on which that right of appeal expires.

(4) If any person—

(a) intentionally obstructs an authorised officer acting in the exercise of the powers conferred to him by regulation 30(4) or (5); or

(b) fails without reasonable excuse to comply with a requirement of an authorised officer pursuant to regulation 30(4) or (5), he shall be guilty of an offence and be liable on summary conviction to a fine not exceeding level 3 on the standard scale.

(5) In this regulation 'requirement' does not include a requirement imposed on an authority or a person acting as arbitrator or arbiter, nor does it include any restriction or obligation in or under regulation 7(5) or (7), 9(1), 11(9), 13(2) or (4) or 16(2).

Notes

Transfer of Functions. Functions of the Minister, in respect of the functions exercisable by the Secretary of State for Wales, transferred to the National Assembly for Wales, by the National Assembly for Wales (Transfer of Functions) Order 1999, SI 1999/672, arts 2, 4, Sch 1.

Confiscation and restoration of quota

32. (1) Within forty-five days after the end of each quota year, each purchaser shall supply to the Intervention Board a list of those producers registered with that purchaser (whether for the whole or part of the quota year) who have not made deliveries to him during that year.

(2) Pursuant to Article 5 of the Council Regulation (which deals with the confiscation and restoration of quota), the Intervention Board shall notify—

    (a)   any producer who from information available to the Intervention Board appears not to have made deliveries or direct sales or a temporary transfer of quota under regulation 13 during the previous quota year, that his quota has been taken into the national reserve;

    (b)   any producer who is a direct seller and to whom the third sub-paragraph of Article 4(2) of the Commission Regulation (which deals with the late submission of declarations) applies that, unless that producer submits to the Intervention Board a declaration under the first sub-paragraph thereof within 30 days of the notification, his quota will be confiscated to the national reserve.

(3) Any quota withdrawn pursuant to Article 5 of the Council Regulation shall be placed in the national reserve with effect from the beginning of the quota year following the quota year for which the list referred to paragraph (1) was supplied, the quota year for which the declaration indicating no direct sales was made, or the quota year for which no declaration was submitted, as the case may be.

(4) Any quota withdrawn pursuant to Article 5 of the Council Regulation may be restored to the producer in respect of the holding from which it was withdrawn within a period of six years from the beginning of the quota year in which it was withdrawn, in accordance with the provisions of this regulation.

(5) A producer who receives a notification of confiscation under paragraph (2) above shall—

    (a)   within 28 days of receipt of that notification notify any person with an interest in the holding of the content of that notification; and

(b) within six months of receipt of that notification, submit a notification to the Intervention Board, in such form as may reasonably be required by the Intervention Board for that purpose, whether he wishes to retain the right to request restoration of the quota and such a notification shall include—

   (i) a statement that he is the occupier of the entirety of the holding and that no other person has an interest in all or any of it;

   (ii) a statement of the agreed apportionment of quota taking account of the areas used for milk production, signed by every person with an interest in the holding; or

   (iii) a statement requesting apportionment of the quota in accordance with an arbitration under paragraphs 1(5), 3, 4 and 6 to 35 of Schedule 2 in respect of England and Wales, paragraphs 1, 2, 3(4) and 5 to 28 of Schedule 3 in respect of Scotland, and paragraphs 1, 2, 3(5), 5, 6, and 8 to 19 of Schedule 4 in respect of Northern Ireland.

(6) Where a producer has notified the Intervention Board under paragraph (5)(b) that he wishes to retain the right to restoration of quota, he may request the Intervention Board to restore to him the quota relating to that holding or part holding provided that the request is submitted to the Intervention Board by 15th July in the quota year following the quota year to which the request relates.

(7) Where a producer has notified the Intervention Board that he wishes to retain the right to restoration of quota and there is a change of occupation of all or part of the holding to which the quota relates, the new occupier may request the Intervention Board to restore to him the quota relating to that holding or part holding, provided that the request is received by the Intervention Board at least six months before the end of the six-year period referred to in paragraph (4) or within six months of the change of occupation, whichever is the earlier.

(8) Where quota is restored to part of a holding in respect of which an apportionment of quota has been made in accordance with or under paragraph 5(b)(ii) or (iii), in accordance with a request made under paragraph (6), or following a change of occupation of part of a holding under paragraph (7), the amount of quota to be restored to that part shall be determined in accordance with—

(a) the apportionment, referred to in paragraph (5)(b)(ii) or (iii) and within that apportionment in proportion to the agricultural areas concerned; or

(b) where no such apportionment has been carried out, in the same proportion which the agricultural area concerned bears to the total agricultural area of the holding from which quota was withdrawn.

(9) Where a producer—

(a) fails to submit a notification in accordance with paragraph (5)(b);

(b) indicates on the notification submitted under paragraph (5)(b) that he does not wish to retain the right to restoration of quota;

(c) fails to request the restoration of quota in accordance with paragraph (6) or (7);

(d) having had quota restored to him in accordance with paragraph (6), fails to make deliveries or direct sales of dairy produce from the holding to which the quota relates within six months after his application for the restoration of quota or the end of the six year period, whichever is the earlier; or

(e) having had quota restored to him following a change of occupation referred to in paragraph (7), fails to make deliveries or direct sales of dairy produce from the holding within eighteen months of the change of occupation or the end of the six year period, whichever is the earlier,

the relevant quota shall be taken into the national reserve.

Withdrawal of Special Quota

33. Where a producer has special quota registered in his name and it appears to the Minister that the producer has made a false or misleading statement in his application for special quota or has failed to comply with the requirements in relation to special quota, the Minister may withdraw the whole or any part of the special quota.

Notes

Transfer of Functions. Functions of the Minister, in respect of the functions exercisable by the Secretary of State for Wales, transferred to the National Assembly for Wales, by the National Assembly for Wales (Transfer of Functions) Order 1999, SI 1999/672, arts 2, 4, Sch 1.

Dairy Produce Quota Tribunals

34. (1) For the purpose of completing the discharge of any functions exercisable by it under the Regulations revoked by these Regulations, the Dairy Produce Quota Tribunal for England and Wales, the Dairy Produce Quota Tribunal for Scotland and the Dairy Produce Quota Tribunal for Northern Ireland constituted under regulation 6 of the 1984 Regulations shall continue in existence and, in respect of a holding situated in more than one area of a Dairy Produce Quota Tribunal, the Dairy Produce Quota Tribunal the functions of which shall relate to that holding shall continue to be the Dairy Produce Quota Tribunal chosen for the purpose by the Ministers.

(2) Schedule 6 shall apply in respect of the constitution, appointment of members, remuneration of members, staffing and procedure of Dairy Produce Quota Tribunals.

Notes

Transfer of Functions. Functions of the Minister, in respect of the functions exercisable by the Secretary of State for Wales, transferred to the National Assembly for Wales, by the National Assembly for Wales (Transfer of Functions) Order 1999, SI 1999/672, arts 2, 4, Sch 1.

Revocation

35. The Dairy Produce Quotas Regulations 1994, the Dairy Produce Quotas (Amendment) Regulations 1994, the Dairy Produce Quotas (Amendment) (No 2) Regulations 1994, the Dairy Produce Quotas (Amendment) Regulations 1995, the Dairy Produce Quotas (Amendment) Regulations 1996 and the Dairy Produce Quotas (Amendment) Regulations 1997 shall be revoked.

SCHEDULE 1

Meaning of Community Legislation

Regulation 2(1)

1. Council Regulation (EEC) No 857/84, adopting general rules for the application of the levy referred to in Article 5c of Regulation (EEC) No 804/68 in the milk and milk products sector, OJ No L90, 1.4.84, p 13.

2. Council Regulation (EEC) No 764/89, amending Regulation (EEC) No 857/84, OJ No L84, 29.3.89, p 2.

3. Council Regulation (EEC) No 1639/91, amending Regulation (EEC) No 857/84, OJ No L150, 15.6.91, p 35.

4. Commission Regulation (EEC) No 1756/93, fixing the operative events for the agricultural conversion rate applicable to milk and milk products, OJ No L161, 2.7.93, p 48.

5. Council Regulation (EEC) No 2187/93, providing for an offer of compensation to certain producers of milk and milk products temporarily prevented from carrying on their trade, OJ No L196, 5.8.93, p 6.

6. Commission Regulation (EEC) No 2562/93, laying down detailed rules for the application of Council Regulation 2055/93, OJ No L235, 18.9.93, p 18.

7. Commission Regulation (EEC) No 2648/93, laying down detailed rules for the application of Council Regulation (EEC) No 2187/93, OJ No L243, 29.9.93, p 1.

SCHEDULE 2

Apportionments and Prospective Apportionments by Arbitration—England and Wales

Regulations 8, 9, 10, and 32

1. *Appointment and remuneration of arbitrator*
(1) In any case where an apportionment is to be carried out by arbitration an arbitrator shall be appointed by agreement between the transferor and transferee within the period of 28 days referred to in regulation 7(1)(a) (referred to in this paragraph as 'the relevant period') and the transferee shall give notice of the appointment of the arbitrator to the Intervention Board within fourteen days of the date of the appointment.

(2) Notwithstanding sub-paragraph (1), the transferor or the transferee may at any time within the relevant period make an application to the President of the Royal Institution of Chartered Surveyors (referred to in this Schedule as 'the President') for the appointment of an arbitrator from amongst the members of the panel referred to in paragraph 8 and the person who makes such an application to the President shall give notice of that fact to the Intervention Board within fourteen days of the date of the application.

(3) If at the expiry of the relevant period an arbitrator has not been appointed by agreement between the transferor and the transferee and no application has been made to the President under sub-paragraph (2), the Intervention Board shall make an application to the President for the appointment of an arbitrator.

(4) Where the Intervention Board gives a notice in accordance with regulation 10 it shall make an application to the President for the appointment of an arbitrator and the Intervention Board shall be a party to the arbitration.

(5) Where an apportionment under regulation 32(5) is to be carried out by arbitration, the producer shall either appoint by agreement with all persons with an interest in the holding or make an application to the President for the appointment of an arbitrator from amongst the members of the panel referred to in paragraph 8.

2. (1) In any case where a prospective apportionment is to be made by arbitration an arbitrator shall be appointed—

    (a) where regulation 10 applies, by the President,
    (b) in any other case, by agreement between the occupier of the relevant holding and any other interested party, or, in default, by the President on an application by the occupier.

(2)   Where sub-paragraph (1)(b) applies, the occupier shall give notice to the Intervention Board of the appointment of the arbitrator pursuant to the agreement, or of the application to the President for the appointment of an arbitrator, within fourteen days of the date of the appointment of the arbitrator or the date of the application to the President, as the case may be.

3. (1) An arbitrator appointed in accordance with paragraphs 1(1) to (4) and 2 shall conduct the arbitration in accordance with this Schedule and shall base his award on findings made by him as to areas used for milk production in the last five year period during which production took place before the change of occupation, or in the case of a prospective apportionment in the last five year period during which production took place before the appointment of the arbitrator.

(2) An arbitrator appointed in accordance with paragraph 1(5) shall conduct the arbitration in accordance with this Schedule and shall base his award on findings made by him as to the areas used for milk production in the last five-year period during which production took place.

(3) An arbitrator appointed under any paragraph of this Schedule shall base his award on findings made by him in accordance with the law in force at the time the event giving rise to an application for arbitration took place.

4. (1) No application may be made to the President for an arbitrator to be appointed by him under this Schedule unless the application is accompanied by the prescribed fee for such an application; but once the fee has been paid in connection with any such application no further fee shall be payable in connection with any subsequent application for the President to exercise any function exercisable by him in relation to the arbitration by virtue of this Schedule (including an application for the appointment by him in an appropriate case of a new arbitrator).

(2) The prescribed fee for the purposes of this paragraph shall be that which from time to time is prescribed as the fee payable to the President under paragraph 1(2) of Schedule 11 to the Agricultural Holdings Act 1986.

5. Where the Intervention Board makes an application to the President under paragraphs 1(3) or (4), the fee payable to the President in respect of that application referred to in paragraph 4 shall be recoverable by the Intervention Board as a debt due from the other parties to the arbitration jointly or severally.

6. Any appointment of an arbitrator by the President shall be made by him as soon as possible after receiving the application.

7. A person appointed by the President as arbitrator shall, where the arbitration relates to a holding in Wales, and any party to the arbitration so requires, be a person who possesses a knowledge of the Welsh language.

8. For the purposes of paragraph 1(2) the panel of arbitrators shall be the panel appointed by the Lord Chancellor under paragraph 1(5) of Schedule 11 to the Agricultural Holdings Act 1986.

9. If the arbitrator dies, or is incapable of acting, or for seven days after notice from any party requiring him to act fails to act, a new arbitrator may be appointed as if no arbitrator had been appointed.

10. No party to the arbitration shall have power to revoke the appointment of the arbitrator without the consent of any other party, and his appointment shall not be revoked by the death of any party.

11. Every appointment, application, notice, revocation and consent under paragraphs 1 to 10 must be in writing.

12. The remuneration of the arbitrator shall be—

(a) where he is appointed by agreement between the parties, such amount as may be agreed upon by him and the parties or, in default of agreement, fixed by the registrar of the county court (subject to an appeal to the judge of the court) on an application made by the arbitrator or any party;

(b) where he is appointed by the President, such amount as may be agreed upon by the arbitrator and the parties or, in default of agreement, fixed by the President,

and shall be recoverable by the arbitrator as a debt due from the parties to the arbitration, jointly or severally.

Conduct of proceedings and witnesses

13. (1) In any arbitration to which this Schedule applies, the arbitrator may, in his absolute discretion, subject to sub-paragraph (2), join as a party to the arbitration any person having an interest in the holding, whether or not such person has applied to become a party to the arbitration, provided that such person consents to be so joined.

(2) Where an apportionment under regulation 32(5) is to be carried out by arbitration, any person with an interest in the holding who has refused to sign the statement referred to in regulation 32(5)(b)(ii) shall be a party to the arbitration.

14. The parties to the arbitration shall, within thirty-five days of the appointment of the arbitrator, or within such further period as the arbitrator may determine, deliver to him a statement of their respective cases with all necessary particulars and—

(a) no amendment or addition to the statement or particulars delivered shall be allowed after the expiry of the said thirty-five days except with the consent of the arbitrator; and

(b) a party to the arbitration shall be confined at the hearing to the matters alleged in the statement and particulars delivered by him and any amendment or addition duly made.

15. The parties to the arbitration and all persons claiming through them shall, subject to any legal objection, submit to be examined by the arbitrator, on oath or affirmation, in relation to the matters in dispute and shall, subject to any such objection, produce before the arbitrator all samples and documents within their possession or power which may be required or called for, and do such other things as the arbitrator reasonably may require for the purposes of the arbitration.

16. Any person having an interest in the holding to which the arbitration relates shall be entitled to make representations to the arbitrator.

17. Witnesses appearing at the arbitration shall, if the arbitrator thinks fit, be examined on oath or affirmation, and the arbitrator shall have power to administer oaths to, or to take the affirmation of, the parties and witnesses appearing.

18. The provisions of county court rules as to the issuing of witness summonses shall, subject to such modifications as may be prescribed by such rules, apply for the purposes of the arbitration as if it were an action or matter in the county court.

19. (1) Subject to sub-paragraphs (2) and (3), any person who—

    (a) having been summoned in pursuance of county court rules as a witness in the arbitration refuses or neglects, without sufficient cause, to appear or to produce any documents required by the summons to be produced, or

    (b) having been so summoned or being present at the arbitration and being required to give evidence, refuses to be sworn or give evidence,

shall forfeit such fine as the judge of the county court may direct.

(2) A judge shall not have power under sub-paragraph (1) above to direct that a person shall forfeit a fine of an amount exceeding £400.

(3) No person summoned in pursuance of county court rules as a witness in the arbitration shall forfeit a fine under this paragraph unless there has been paid or tendered to him at the time of the service of the summons such sum in respect of his expenses (including, in such cases as may be prescribed by county court rules, compensation for loss of time) as may be so prescribed for the purposes of section 55 of the County Courts Act 1984.

(4) The judge of the county court may at his discretion direct that the whole or any part of any such fine, after deducting costs, shall be applicable towards indemnifying the party injured by the refusal or neglect.

20. (1) Subject to sub-paragraph (2), the judge of the county court may, if he thinks fit, upon application on affidavit by any party to the arbitration, issue an order under his hand for bringing up before the arbitrator any person (in this paragraph referred to as a 'prisoner') confined in any place under any sentence or under committal for trial or otherwise, to be examined as a witness in the arbitration.

(2) No such order shall be made with respect to a person confined under process in any civil action or matter.

(3) Subject to sub-paragraph (4), the prisoner mentioned in any such order shall be brought before the arbitrator under the same custody, and shall be dealt with in the same manner in all respects, as a prisoner required

by a writ of habeas corpus to be brought before the High Court and examined there as a witness.

(4) The person having the custody of the prisoner shall not be bound to obey the order unless there is tendered to him a reasonable sum for the conveyance and maintenance of a proper officer or officers and of the prisoner in going to, remaining at, and returning from, the place where the arbitration is held.

21. The High Court may order that a writ of habeas corpus ad testificandum shall issue to bring up a prisoner for examination before the arbitrator, if the prisoner is confined in any prison under process in any civil action or matter.

Award

22. (1) Subject to sub-paragraph (2), the arbitrator shall make and sign his award within fifty-six days of his appointment.

(2) The President may from time to time enlarge the time limited for making the award, whether that time has expired or not.

(3) The arbitrator shall notify the terms of his award to the Intervention Board within eight days of delivery of that award.

(4) The award shall fix a date not later than one month after the delivery of the award for the payment of any costs awarded under paragraph 26.

23. The award shall be final and binding on the parties and any persons claiming under them.

24. The arbitrator shall have power to correct in the award any clerical mistake or error arising from any accidental slip or omission.

Reasons for award

25. Where the arbitrator is requested by any party to the arbitration, on or before the making of the award, to make a statement, either written or oral, of the reasons for the award, the arbitrator shall furnish such a statement.

Costs

26. The costs of and incidental to the arbitration and award shall be in the discretion of the arbitrator who may direct to and by whom and in what manner the costs, or any part of the costs, are to be paid. The costs for the purposes of this paragraph shall include any fee paid to the President in respect of the appointment of an arbitrator and any sum paid to the Intervention Board pursuant to paragraph 5.

27. On the application of any party, any such costs shall be taxable in the county court according to such of the scales prescribed by county court rules for proceedings in the county court as may be directed by the arbitrator under paragraph 26, or, in the absence of any such direction, by the county court.

28. (1) The arbitrator shall, in awarding costs, take into consideration—

   (a) the reasonableness or unreasonableness of the claim of any party, whether in respect of the amount or otherwise,

   (b) any unreasonable demand for particulars or refusal to supply particulars, and

   (c) generally all the circumstances of the case.

(2) The arbitrator may disallow any costs which he considers to have been unnecessarily incurred, including the costs of any witness whom he considers to have been called unnecessarily.

Special case, setting aside award and remission

29. The arbitrator may at any stage of the proceedings and shall, upon a direction in that behalf given by the judge of the county court upon an application made by any party, state in the form of a special case for the opinion of the county court any question of law arising in the course of the arbitration and any question as to the jurisdiction of the arbitrator.

30. (1) Where the arbitrator has misconducted himself, the county court may remove him.

(2) Where the arbitrator has misconducted himself, or an arbitration or award has been improperly procured, or there is an error of law on the face of the award, the county court may set the award aside.

31. (1) The county court may from time to time remit the award, or any part of the award, to the reconsideration of the arbitrator.

(2) In any case where it appears to the county court that there is an error of law on the face of the award, the court may, instead of exercising its power of remission under sub-paragraph (1), vary the award by substituting for so much of it as is affected by the error such award as the court considers that it would have been proper for the arbitrator to make in the circumstances; and the award shall thereupon have effect as so varied.

(3) Where remission is ordered under that sub-paragraph, the arbitrator shall, unless the order otherwise directs, make and sign his award within thirty days of the date of the order.

(4) If the county court is satisfied that the time limited for making the said award is for any good reason insufficient, the court may extend or further extend that time for such period as it thinks proper.

Miscellaneous

32. Any amount paid, in respect of the remuneration of the arbitrator by any party to the arbitration in excess of the amount, if any, directed by the award to be paid by him in respect of the costs of the award, shall be recoverable from the other party or jointly from the other parties.

33. For the purposes of this Schedule, an arbitrator appointed by the

President shall be taken to have been so appointed at the time when the President executed the instrument of appointment, in accordance with the law in force at the time of such execution and in the case of any such arbitrator the periods mentioned in paragraphs 14 and 22 shall accordingly run from that time.

34. Any instrument of appointment or other document purporting to be made in the exercise of any function exercisable by the President under paragraph 1, 2, 6, 7, 12 or 22 and to be signed by or on behalf of the President shall be taken to be such an instrument or document unless the contrary is shown.

35. The Arbitration Act 1996 shall not apply to an arbitration determined in accordance with this Schedule.

SCHEDULE 3

Apportionments and Prospective Apportionments by Arbitration or Scottish Land Court Scotland

Regulations 8, 9, 10 and 32

Part I

General

1. (1) Subject to sub-paragraphs (2) and (3) below, all apportionments and prospective apportionments in respect of holdings in Scotland shall be carried out by arbitration and the provisions of Part II of this Schedule shall apply.

(2) The Scottish Land Court shall carry out the apportionment or prospective apportionment where the holding or any part of the holding constitutes or, immediately prior to the transfer giving rise to the apportionment, constituted—

(a) a croft within the meaning of section 3 of the Crofters (Scotland) Act 1993;

(b) a holding within the meaning of section 2 of the Small Landholders (Scotland) Act 1911; or

(c) the holding of a statutory small tenant under section 32 of the Small Landholders (Scotland) Act 1911.

(3) Where sub-paragraph (2) above does not apply and the holding or any part of the holding constitutes or, immediately prior to the transfer giving rise to the apportionment, constituted an agricultural holding within the meaning of section 1 of the Agricultural Holdings (Scotland) Act 1991, the Scottish Land Court shall carry out the apportionment or prospective apportionment if requested to do so by a joint application of all parties interested in the apportionment, made within the period of 28 days referred to in regulation 7(1)(a).

(4) Where the Scottish Land Court carries out any apportionment or prospective apportionment, Part III of this Schedule shall apply.

2. (1) An arbiter or the Scottish Land Court, as the case may be, shall decide the apportionment on the basis of findings made as to areas used for milk production in the last five-year period during which production took place before the change of occupation or, in the case of a prospective apportionment, in the last five-year period during which production took place before the appointment of the arbiter or the application to the Scottish Land Court.

(2) Notwithstanding sub-paragraph (1), an arbiter appointed in accordance with paragraph 3(4) shall conduct the arbitration in accordance with this Schedule and shall base his award on findings made by him as to the areas used for milk production in the last five year period during which production took place.

Part II

Apportionments Carried Out by Arbitration

Appointment and remuneration of arbiter

3. (1) In any case where the apportionment is to be carried out by arbitration, an arbiter shall be appointed by agreement between the transferor and transferee within the period of 28 days referred to in regulation 7(1)(a) (referred to in this paragraph as 'the relevant period') and the transferee shall give notice of the appointment of the arbiter to the Minister within fourteen days from the date of the appointment.

(2) Notwithstanding sub-paragraph (1), the transferor or the transferee may at any time within the relevant period make an application to the Minister for the appointment of an arbiter.

(3) If at the expiry of the relevant period an arbiter has not been appointed by agreement between the transferor and the transferee nor an application made to the Minister under sub-paragraph (2), the Minister shall at his own instance proceed to appoint an arbiter.

(4) Where an apportionment under regulation 32(5) is to be carried out by arbitration, the producer shall either appoint an arbiter with the agreement of all persons with an interest in the holding or make an application to the Minister for the appointment of an arbiter.

4. (1) In any case where a prospective apportionment is to be made by arbitration, an arbiter shall be appointed by agreement between the occupier and any other interested party or, in default of agreement, by the Minister on an application by the occupier.

(2) Where an arbiter is appointed by agreement in terms of sub-paragraph (1), the occupier shall give notice of the appointment of the arbiter to the Minister within fourteen days from the date of the appointment.

5. (1) Where, in terms of a notice given by the Intervention Board under regulation 10, an apportionment or prospective apportionment is to be carried out by arbitration, the Intervention Board shall apply to the Scottish Land Court for the appointment of an arbiter.

(2) Any fee payable by the Intervention Board on an application to the Scottish Land Court under sub-paragraph (1) shall be recoverable by it as a debt due from the other parties to the arbitration jointly or severally.

(3) Where the Minister is to be a party to an arbitration (otherwise than in terms of a notice given under regulation 10), the arbiter shall, in lieu of being appointed by the Minister, be appointed by the Scottish Land Court.

6. If the person appointed arbiter dies, or is incapable of acting, or for seven days after notice from any party requiring him to act fails to act, a new arbiter may be appointed as if no arbiter had been appointed.

7. No party to the arbitration shall have power to revoke the appointment of the arbiter without the consent of any other party.

8. Every appointment, application, notice, revocation and consent under paragraphs 1 to 7 must be in writing.

9. The remuneration of the arbiter shall be—

   (a)   where he is appointed by agreement between the parties, such amount as may be agreed upon by him and the parties or, in default of agreement, fixed by the auditor of the sheriff court (subject to an appeal to the sheriff) on an application made by the arbiter or one of the parties;
   (b)   where he is appointed by the Minister, such amount as may be fixed by the Minister;
   (c)   where he is appointed by the Scottish Land Court, such amount as may be fixed by that Court;

and shall be recoverable by the arbiter as a debt due from any one of the parties to the arbitration.

Conduct of proceedings and witnesses

10. The parties to the arbitration shall within twenty-eight days of the appointment of the arbiter deliver to him a statement of their respective cases with all necessary particulars; and—

   (a)   no amendment or addition to the statement or particulars delivered shall be allowed after the expiry of the said twenty-eight days except with the consent of the arbiter;
   (b)   a party to the arbitration shall be confined at the hearing to the matters alleged in the statement and particulars delivered by him and any amendment or addition duly made.

11. The parties to the arbitration, and all persons claiming through them, shall, subject to any legal objection, submit to be examined by the arbiter on oath or affirmation in relation to the matters in dispute and shall, subject to any such objection, produce before the arbiter all samples, books, deeds, papers, accounts, writings and documents, within their possession or power which may be required or called for, and do all other things as the arbiter reasonably may require for the purposes of the arbitration.

12. Any person having an interest in the holding to which the arbitration relates shall be entitled to make representations to the arbiter. The Intervention Board may make such representations where the arbitration follows on a notice given by it under regulation 10.

13. The arbiter shall have power to administer oaths, and to take the affirmation of parties and witnesses appearing, and witnesses shall, if the arbiter thinks fit, be examined on oath or affirmation.

Award

14. (1) The arbiter shall make and sign his award within three months of his appointment or within such longer period as may, either before or after the expiry of the aforesaid period, be agreed to in writing by the parties or fixed by the Minister.

(2) The arbiter shall notify the terms of his award to the Minister within eight days of the delivery of that award.

(3) The award shall fix a date not later than one month after the delivery of the award for the payment of any expenses awarded under paragraph 17.

15. The award to be made by the arbiter shall be final and binding on the parties and the persons claiming under them respectively.

16. The arbiter may correct in an award any clerical mistake or error arising from any accidental slip or omission.

Expenses

17. The expenses of and incidental to the arbitration and award shall be in the discretion of the arbiter, who may direct to and by whom and in what manner those expenses or any part thereof are to be paid, and the expenses shall be subject to taxation by the auditor of the sheriff court on the application of any party, but that taxation shall be subject to review by the sheriff.

18. (1) The arbiter shall, in awarding expenses, take into consideration—

(a) the reasonableness or unreasonableness of the claim of any party, whether in respect of amount or otherwise;
(b) any unreasonable demand for particulars or refusal to supply particulars; and
(c) generally all the circumstances of the case.

(2) The arbiter may disallow any expenses which he considers to have been incurred unnecessarily, including the expenses of any witness whom he considers to have been called unnecessarily.

19. It shall not be lawful to include in the expenses of and incidental to the arbitration and award, or to charge against any of the parties, any sum payable in respect of remuneration or expenses to any person appointed by the arbiter to act as clerk or otherwise to assist him in the arbitration unless such appointment was made after submission of the claim and answers to the arbiter and with either the consent of the parties to the arbitration or the sanction of the sheriff.

Statement of case

20. The arbiter may at any stage of the proceedings, and shall, if so directed by the sheriff (which direction may be given on the application of any party), state a case for the opinion of the sheriff on any questions of law arising in the course of the arbitration. The opinion of the sheriff on any case shall be final.

Removal of arbiter and setting aside of award

21. Where an arbiter has misconducted himself the sheriff may remove him.

22. When an arbiter has misconducted himself, or an arbitration or award has been improperly procured, the sheriff may set the award aside.

Miscellaneous

23. Any amount paid in respect of the remuneration of the arbiter by any party to the arbitration in excess of the amount, if any, directed by the award to be paid by him in respect of the expenses of the award shall be recoverable from the other party or jointly from the other parties.

24. The Arbitration (Scotland) Act 1894 shall not apply to any arbitration carried out under this Schedule.

Notes

Transfer of Functions. Functions of the Minister, in respect of the functions exercisable by the Secretary of State for Wales, transferred to the National Assembly for Wales, by the National Assembly for Wales (Transfer of Functions) Order 1999, SI 1999/672, arts 2, 4, Sch 1.

Part III

Apportionments Carried Out by the Scottish Land Court

25. The provisions of the Small Landholders (Scotland) Acts 1886 to 1931 with regard to the Scottish Land Court shall, with any necessary modifications, apply for the purpose of the determination of any matter which they are required, in terms of paragraph 1, to determine, in like manner as those provisions apply for the purpose of the determination by the Land Court of matters referred to them under those Acts.

26. Where an apportionment or prospective apportionment is to be dealt with by the Scottish Land Court, the party making application to that Court shall notify the Minister in writing of the application within fourteen days of its being lodged with the Court.

27. Where, in terms of a notice given by the Intervention Board under regulation 10, an apportionment or prospective apportionment is to be carried out by the Scottish Land Court, any fee payable by the Intervention Board to the Court shall be recoverable by it as a debt due from the other parties to the case jointly or severally.

28. Any person having an interest in the holding to which the apportionment or prospective apportionment relates shall be entitled to be a party to the proceedings before the Scottish Land Court. The Intervention Board shall be entitled to be a party where the apportionment follows on a notice given by it under regulation 10.

SCHEDULE 4

Apportionments and Prospective Apportionments by Arbitration— Northern Ireland

Regulations 8, 9, 10 and 32

1. Paragraphs 3 to 19 shall apply to every arbitration in Northern Ireland.

2. (1) Parts I, II and IV of the Arbitration Act 1996 shall, except insofar as they are inconsistent with paragraphs 3 to 19, apply to every arbitration in Northern Ireland as if that arbitration were pursuant to an arbitration agreement and as if paragraphs 3 to 11 and 13 to 18 were contained in an arbitration agreement.

(2) For the purposes of this paragraph 'arbitration agreement' shall be construed in accordance with sections 5(1) and 6 of the Arbitration Act 1996.

Appointment of arbitrator

3. (1) In any case where an apportionment is to be carried out by arbitration an arbitrator shall be appointed by agreement between the transferor and transferee within the period of 28 days referred to in regulation 7(1)(a) (referred to in this paragraph as 'the relevant period') and the transferee shall give notice of the appointment of the arbitrator to the Intervention Board within fourteen days of the date of the appointment.

(2) Notwithstanding sub-paragraph (1) above, the transferor or the transferee may at any time within the relevant period make an application to the President of the Law Society of Northern Ireland (referred to in this

Schedule as 'the President') for the appointment of an arbitrator and the person who makes such an application to the President shall give notice of that fact to the Intervention Board within fourteen days of the date of the application.

(3) If at the expiry of the relevant period an arbitrator has not been appointed by agreement between the transferor and the transferee nor an application made to the President under sub-paragraph (2), the Intervention Board shall make an application to the President for the appointment of an arbitrator.

(4) Where the Intervention Board gives a notice in accordance with regulation 10 he shall make an application to the President for the appointment of an arbitrator and the Intervention Board shall be a party to the arbitration.

(5) Where an apportionment under regulation 32(5) is to be carried out by arbitration, the producer shall either appoint an arbitrator by agreement with all persons with an interest in the holding or make an application to the President for the appointment of an arbitrator.

4. (1) In any case where a prospective apportionment is to be made by arbitration an arbitrator shall be appointed—

   (a) where regulation 10 applies, by the President;

   (b) in any other case, by agreement between the occupier of the holding to which the prospective apportionment relates and any other interested party, or, in default, by the President on an application by that occupier.

(2) Where sub-paragraph (1)(b) applies, the occupier shall give notice to the Intervention Board of the appointment of the arbitrator pursuant to the agreement, or of the application to the President for the appointment of an arbitrator, within fourteen days of the date of the appointment of the arbitrator or the date of the application to the President, as the case may be.

5. (1) An arbitrator appointed in accordance with paragraphs 3(1) to (4) and 4 shall conduct the arbitration in accordance with this Schedule and shall base his award on findings made by him as to areas used for milk production in the last five year period during which production took place before the change of occupation, or in the case of a prospective apportionment in the last five year period during which production took place before the appointment of the arbitrator.

(2) An arbitrator appointed in accordance with paragraph 3(5) shall conduct the arbitration in accordance with this Schedule and shall base his award on findings made by him as to areas used for milk production in the last five year period during which production took place.

(3) An arbitrator appointed under any paragraph of this Schedule shall base his award on findings made by him in accordance with the law in force at the time the event giving rise to an application for arbitration took place.

6. No application may be made to the President for an arbitrator to be appointed by him under this Schedule unless the application is accompanied by the fee which shall be £50 for such an application; but once the fee has been paid in connection with any such application no further fee shall be payable in connection with any subsequent application for the President to exercise any function exercisable by him in relation to the arbitration by virtue of this Schedule (including an application for the appointment by him in an appropriate case of a new arbitrator).

7. Where the Intervention Board makes an application to the President under paragraph 3(3) or (4), the fee payable to the President in respect of that application referred to in paragraph 6 above shall be recoverable by the Intervention Board as a debt due from the parties to the arbitration jointly or severally.

8. Any appointment of an arbitrator by the President shall be made by him within fourteen days after receiving the application.

9. If the arbitrator dies, or is incapable of acting, or for seven days after notice from any party requiring him to act fails to act, a new arbitrator may be appointed as if no arbitrator had been appointed.

10. A party to the arbitration shall have power to revoke the appointment of the arbitrator with the consent of all other parties.

11. Every appointment, application, notice, revocation and consent under paragraphs 1 to 10 shall be in writing.

Persons with an interest in the holding

12. (1) In an arbitration to which this Schedule applies, the arbitrator may, in his absolute discretion, subject to sub-paragraph (2), join as a party to the arbitration any person having an interest in the holding, whether or not such person has applied to become a party to the arbitration, provided that such person consents to be so joined.

(2) Where an apportionment under regulation 32(5) is to be carried out by arbitration, any person with an interest in the holding who has refused to sign the statement referred to in regulation 32(5)(b)(ii) shall be a party to the arbitration.

Statement of case

13. The parties to the arbitration shall, within thirty-five days of the appointment of the arbitrator, deliver to him a statement of their respective cases with all necessary particulars and—

    (a) no amendment or addition to the statement or particulars delivered shall be allowed after the expiry of the said thirty-five days except with the consent of the arbitrator;

    (b) a party to the arbitration shall be confined at the hearing to the matters alleged in the statement and particulars delivered by him and any amendment or addition duly made.

Award

14. The arbitrator shall make and sign his award within fifty-six days of his appointment.

15. The arbitrator shall notify the terms of his award to the Intervention Board within eight days of the delivery of that award.

16. The arbitrator shall have power to correct in the award any clerical mistake or error arising from any accidental slip or omission.

Reasons for award

17. If requested by any party to the arbitration, on or before the making of the award, to make a statement, either written or oral, of the reasons for the award the arbitrator shall furnish such a statement.

18. For the purposes of this Schedule, an arbitrator appointed by the President shall be taken to have been so appointed at the time when the President executed the instrument of appointment; and in the case of any such arbitrator the periods mentioned in paragraphs 13 and 14 shall run from that time.

19. Any person having an interest in the holding to which the arbitration relates shall be entitled to make representations to the arbitrator.

SCHEDULE 5

Reallocation of Quota and Calculation of Levy Liability

Regulation 18

Wholesale quota

1. The Intervention Board shall determine the amount, if any, by which the wholesale deliveries of dairy produce to each purchaser exceeds his purchaser quota.

2. In making that determination the Intervention Board shall complete in sequence the steps required by paragraphs 3 to 7.

3. The Intervention Board shall where necessary authorise an adjustment of the amount, if any, by which the quantity of wholesale deliveries of dairy produce to each purchaser must be adjusted to take account of its fat content, calculated in accordance with Article 2(2) of the Commission Regulation.

4. The Intervention Board shall authorise the adjustment by purchasers (to the extent possible from within the quota available to the purchaser to whom the producer makes deliveries) of the quota of any producer making wholesale deliveries to whom a temporary reallocation of quota has been made, to take account of that reallocation, in accordance with the order of priority set out in regulation 14(7) and any purchaser who has insufficient quota unused by producers registered with him to meet that temporary reallocation shall notify the Intervention Board of the amount of the shortfall in such form as may reasonably be required by the Intervention Board.

5. The Intervention Board shall determine for each purchaser the amount, if any, by which the purchaser quota of each purchaser exceeds or falls short of the quantity of wholesale deliveries of dairy produce made to him taking into account the amount of quota converted in accordance with regulation 16, and any temporary reallocation made in accordance with paragraph 4.

6. The Intervention Board shall determine the total amount, if any, of excess quota remaining for any purchaser whose purchaser quota exceeds the quantity of wholesale deliveries of dairy produce made to him, as determined in accordance with paragraph 5, and shall add that amount to the national reserve.

7. The Intervention Board shall reallocate the amount, if any, referred to in paragraph 6—

    (a) in the first instance, to meet any award of a temporary realloca-tion of quota which has not been met by the adjustment referred to in paragraph 4 above in accordance with the order of priority set out in regulation 14(7);

    (b) thereafter, to offset the amount by which the deliveries made to any purchaser exceed his purchaser quota, such allocation being made proportionately to the amount of quota; and

    (c) where the allocations referred to in sub-paragraph (b) exceed the amount required by the purchaser, the surplus shall be allocated to all purchasers where the deliveries exceed purchaser quota, until all unallocated quota has been exhausted.

8. Where a purchaser fails to notify the Intervention Board within 45 days of the end of the quota year of the actual quantity of milk or milk products delivered to him in that year, the Intervention Board may decide that that purchaser shall not benefit from the reallocation of quota referred to in paragraph 7(b).

9. The Intervention Board shall determine the total amount of the levy payable by a purchaser by multiplying the amount, if any, by which deliv-eries to him exceed his purchaser quota following the steps specified in paragraphs 3 to 7 by the rate of levy calculated in accordance with Article 1 of the Council Regulation.

10. Where, for any quota year, a purchaser is unable to supply such proof of the quantities of dairy produce delivered to him that year as the Intervention Board may reasonably require, the Intervention Board shall make its own determination of those quantities, based on all the information available to it, for the purposes of calculating any levy payable by that purchaser, and shall inform the purchaser of such determination.

Direct sales quota

11. The Intervention Board shall determine for each direct seller the amount, if any, after taking into account the amount of quota converted in accordance with regulation 16, by which his direct sales quota exceeds the quantity of dairy produce sold by direct sale by him, and shall add this to any quantities available in the national reserve.

12. The Intervention Board shall make an award of a temporary reallocation of direct sales quota, under the terms of regulation 14, and in accordance with the order of priority set out in regulation 14(7) from the aggregate of amounts, if any, referred to in paragraph 11.

13. The Intervention Board shall determine the aggregate amount, if any, by which the direct sales quota of all direct sellers falls short of the total quantity of dairy produce sold by direct sales by them, after taking into account the amount of quota converted in accordance with regulation 16, and any temporary reallocation made in accordance with paragraph 12.

14. The Intervention Board shall determine for each direct seller the amount, if any, by which his direct sales quota falls short of the quantity of dairy produce sold by direct sale by him, taking into account the amount of quota converted in accordance with regulation 16, and any temporary reallocation of quota made in accordance with paragraph 12.

15. The Intervention Board shall determine the aggregate of the amounts, if any, referred to in paragraph 14.

16. The Intervention Board shall determine the total amount of the levy payable by multiplying the amount, if any, referred to in paragraph 13 by the rate of levy calculated in accordance with Article 1 of the Council Regulation.

17. The Intervention Board shall calculate the rate of levy per litre, if any, to be paid by each direct seller on the amount, if any, at paragraph 14 by dividing the amount calculated in accordance with paragraph 16 by the aggregate referred to in paragraph 15.

18. Where a direct seller fails to notify the Intervention Board within 45 days of the end of the quota year of the total quantity of milk products sold by him by direct sales in that year, the Intervention Board may require that the rate of levy per litre to be paid by that direct seller on the quantity not notified shall be the rate calculated in accordance with Article 1 of the Council Regulation.

19. Where for any quota year a direct seller is unable to supply such proof as the Intervention Board may reasonably require of the quantities of dairy produce sold by him in that year, the Intervention Board shall make its own determination of those quantities, based on all the information available to it, for the purposes of calculating any levy payable by that direct seller, and shall inform the direct seller of its determination.

SCHEDULE 6

Dairy Produce Quota Tribunals

Regulation 34

Part 1

Dairy Produce Quota Tribunals (Other Than for Scotland)

1. Each Dairy Produce Quota Tribunal shall consist of up to ninety members appointed by the Minister. The Minister shall designate one of the members of each Tribunal as the Chairman of that Tribunal and may, if he thinks fit, designate another member as the Deputy Chairman.

2. The quorum for any determination by a Dairy Produce Quota Tribunal shall be three.

3. Any determination to be made by a Dairy Produce Quota Tribunal shall be made by a majority.

4. Each Dairy Produce Quota Tribunal may be serviced by a Secretary and such other staff as the Minister may appoint.

5. Any document purporting to be signed by the Chairman or Deputy Chairman of, or the Secretary to, a Dairy Produce Quota Tribunal and purporting to state a determination (or guidance) of the Dairy Produce Quota Tribunal shall in any proceedings be evidence of such a determination (or such guidance).

6. The terms of appointment and the remuneration of the members, Secretary and other staff of a Dairy Produce Quota Tribunal shall be determined by the Minister.

7. Except as otherwise provided in these Regulations, the procedure of a Dairy Produce Quota Tribunal shall be such as the Chairman or, in the absence of the Chairman, the Deputy Chairman shall determine.

Notes
   Transfer of Functions. Functions of the Minister, in respect of the functions exercisable by the Secretary of State for Wales, transferred to the National Assembly for Wales, by the National Assembly for Wales (Transfer of Functions) Order 1999, SI 1999/672, arts 2, 4, Sch 1.

Part II

The Dairy Produce Quota Tribunal for Scotland

8. The Dairy Produce Quota Tribunal shall consist of up to twenty members appointed by the Minister.

9. The Dairy Produce Quota Tribunal shall sit in separate panels, and a determination of any such panel shall be treated as the determination of the Tribunal for the purpose of these Regulations.

10. Each panel constituted under paragraph 9 shall choose their own Chairman.

11. The quorum for any determination by the Dairy Produce Quota Tribunal shall be three.

12. Any determination to be made by the Dairy Produce Quota Tribunal shall be made by a majority.

13. Each panel constituted under paragraph 9 shall be serviced by a Secretary and such other staff as the Minister may appoint.

14. Any document purporting to be signed by the Chairman of or the Secretary to a panel constituted under paragraph 9 and purporting to state a determination of the Dairy Produce Quota Tribunal shall in any proceedings be evidence of such a determination.

15. The terms of appointment and the remuneration of—

(a)   the members of the Dairy Produce Quota Tribunal, and
(b)   the Secretary and other staff of a panel constituted under paragraph 9 shall be determined by the Minister.

16. Except as otherwise provided in these Regulations, the procedure of a panel constituted under paragraph 9 shall be such as their Chairman shall in his discretion determine.

17. A panel constituted under paragraph 9 may consult with any person whom the panel consider to be capable of assisting them in reaching their determination and, in the event of such consultation, the applicant whose special case claim under the Regulations revoked by these Regulations is being examined by the panel shall be afforded the opportunity to comment, before the panel reach their determination, on any advice given by that person.

Part III

General

18. The Dairy Produce Quota Tribunals for England and Wales, Scotland and Northern Ireland shall, if so required by the Minister, issue a joint written statement of general guidance in respect of the criteria to be used in reaching any determination and each Dairy Produce Quota Tribunal shall make its determinations in accordance with those criteria.

Notes
   Transfer of Functions. Functions of the Minister, in respect of the functions exercisable by the Secretary of State for Wales, transferred to the National Assembly for Wales, by the National Assembly for Wales (Transfer of Functions) Order 1999, SI 1999/672, arts 2, 4, Sch 1.

AGRICULTURAL HOLDINGS (UNITS OF PRODUCTION) (ENGLAND) ORDER 1999

SI 1999/2230

The Minister of Agriculture, Fisheries and Food, being the Minister designated in relation to England for the purposes of paragraph 4 of Schedule 6 to the Agricultural Holdings Act 1986, and of all other powers enabling him in that behalf, hereby makes the following Order:—

Title, commencement and interpretation

1. (1) This Order may be cited as the Agricultural Holdings (Units of Production) (England) Order 1999 and shall come into force on 12th September 1999.

   (2) Any reference in this Order to 'the Schedule' is a reference to the Schedule to this Order.

   (3) Any reference in this Order to a Community instrument is a reference to that instrument and any amendment of such instrument in force on the date this Order is made.

   (4) In this Order:

   'Council Regulation 805/68' means Council Regulation (EEC) No 805/68 on the common organisation of the market in beef and veal;
   'Council Regulation 1765/92' means Council Regulation (EEC) No 1765/92 establishing a support system for producers of certain arable crops;
   'Council Regulation 2467/98' means Council Regulation (EC) No 2467/98 on the common organisation of the market in sheepmeat and goatmeat;
   'Council Regulation 1251/99' means Council Regulation (EC) No

1251/99 establishing a support system for producers of certain arable crops;

'Council Regulation 1254/99' means Council Regulation (EC) No 1254/99 on the common organisation of the market in beef and veal.

Assessment of productive capacity of land

2. (1) Paragraphs (2) and (3) of this article have effect for the purpose of the assessment of the productive capacity of a unit of agricultural land situated in England, in order to determine whether that unit is a commercial unit of agricultural land within the meaning of sub-paragraph (1) of paragraph 3 of Schedule 6 to the Agricultural Holdings Act 1986.

(2) Where the land in question is capable, when farmed under competent management, of being used to produce any livestock, crop, fruit, etc, as is mentioned in any of the entries 1 to 7 in column 1 of the Schedule, then—

(a) the unit of production prescribed in relation to that use of the land shall be the unit specified in column 2 of the Schedule opposite to that entry, and

(b) the amount determined, for the period of 12 months beginning with 12th September 1999, as the net annual income from that unit of production in that period shall be the amount specified in column 3 of the Schedule opposite that unit of production.

(3) Where land capable, when farmed under competent management, of producing a net annual income is designated as set aside land, as is mentioned in entry 8 in column 1 of the Schedule, then—

(a) the unit of production prescribed in relation to that use of the land shall be the unit specified in column 2 of the Schedule opposite to that entry, and

(b) the amount determined, for the period of 12 months beginning with 12th September 1999, as the net annual income from that unit of production in that period shall be the amount specified in column 3 of the Schedule opposite that unit of production.

(4) The Schedule has effect subject to the Notes to the Schedule.

Partial Revocation

3. The Agricultural Holdings (Units of Production) Order 1998 is hereby revoked with respect to land situated in England.

SCHEDULE: PRESCRIBED UNITS OF PRODUCTION AND
DETERMINATION OF NET ANNUAL INCOME

Articles 1(2) and 2

Column 1	*Column 2*	*Column 3*
Farming use	Unit of production	Net annual income from unit of production £
1. *Livestock*		
Dairy cows:		
Channel Islands breeds	cow	283
Other breeds	cow	335
Beef breeding cows:		
On eligible land under the Hill Livestock (Compensatory Allowances) Regulations 1996	cow	50(1)
On other land	cow	41(1)
Beef fattening cattle (semi-intensive)	head	48(2)
Dairy replacements	head	41(3)
Ewes:		
On eligible land under the Hill Livestock (Compensatory Allowances) Regulations 1996	ewe	20(4)
On other land	ewe	21(5)
Store lambs (including ewe lambs sold as shearlings)	head	0.87
Pigs:		
Sows and gilts in pig	sow or gilt	90
Porker	head	2.06
Cutter	head	3.66
Bacon	head	5.13
Poultry:		
Laying hens	bird	1.08
Broilers	bird	0.12
Point-of-lay pulllets	bird	0.27
Turkeys	bird	1.23
2. *Farm arable crops*		
Barley	hectare	158(6)
Beans	hectare	75(7)
Herbage seed	hectare	189
Linseed	hectare	137(8)
Oats	hectare	142(9)

Column 1	*Column 2*	*Column 3*
Farming use	Unit of production	Net annual income from unit of production £
Oilseed rape	hectare	164(10)
Peas:		
Dried	hectare	61(11)
Vining	hectare	257
Potatoes:		
First early	hectare	675
Maincrop (including seed)	hectare	790
Sugar Beet	hectare	357
Wheat	hectare	201(12)
3. *Outdoor horticultural crops*		
Broad beans	hectare	409
Brussels sprouts	hectare	1460
Cabbage, savoys and sprouting broccoli	hectare	1684
Carrots	hectare	2307
Cauliflower and winter broccoli	hectare	1017
Celery	hectare	6175
Leeks	hectare	3255
Lettuce	hectare	3914
Onions:		
Dry bulb	hectare	1087
Salad	hectare	4477
Outdoor bulbs	hectare	1416
Parsnips	hectare	2539
Rhubarb (natural)	hectare	3096
Turnips and swedes	hectare	1289
4. *Protected crops*		
Forced narcissi	1000 square metres	8294
Forced tulips	1000 square metres	6226
Mushrooms	1000 square metres	11272
5. *Orchard fruit*		
Apples:		
Cider	hectare	603
Cooking	hectare	1412
Dessert	hectare	1378
Cherries	hectare	1297
Pears	hectare	1100
Plums	hectare	1030

Column 1	Column 2	Column 3
Farming use	Unit of production	Net annual income from unit of production £
6. *Soft fruit*		
Blackcurrants	hectare	1093
Gooseberries	hectare	1579
Raspberries	hectare	2974
Strawberries	hectare	3093
7. *Miscellaneous*		
Hops	hectare	1700
8. *Set aside*[1]	hectare	62

Notes to the Schedule

Article 2(4)

Note to column 1

(1) For the marketing year 1999/2000 this refers to land which is set-aside under Article 2(5) of Council Regulation 1765/92, except where such land is used (in accordance with Article 7(4) of Council Regulation 1765/92) for the provision of materials for the manufacture within the Community of products not primarily intended for human or animal consumption.

From 1st July 2000 this refers to land which is set-aside under Article 2(3) of Council Regulation 1251/99, except where such land is used (in accordance with Article 6(3) of Council Regulation 1251/99) for the provision of materials for the manufacture within the Community of products not primarily intended for human or animal consumption.

Notes to column 3

(1) Deduct £103 from this figure in the case of animals for which the net annual income does not include a sum in respect of the premium for maintaining suckler cows (suckler cow premium) provided for in Article 4d of Council Regulation 805/68 (Article 6 of Council Regulation 1254/99).

Add £26 to the figure in column 3 in the case of animals for which the net annual income includes a sum in respect of the lower rate of extensification premium provided for in Article 4h of Council Regulation 805/68 (Article 13 of Council Regulation 1254/99).

Add £37 to the figure in column 3 in the case of animals for which the net annual income includes a sum in respect of the higher rate of extensification premium provided for in Article 4h of Council Regulation 805/68 (Article 13 of Council Regulation 1254/99).

(2) This is the figure for animals which are kept for 12 months.

Deduct £82 in the case of animals which are kept for 12 months and for which the net annual income does not include a sum in respect of the special premium for holding male bovine animals (beef special premium) provided for in Article 4b of Council Regulation 805/68 (Article 4 of Council Regulation 1254/99).

Add £26 to the figure in column 3 in the case of animals which are kept for 12 months and for which the net annual income includes a sum in respect of the lower rate of extensification premium.

Add £37 to the figure in column 3 in the case of animals which would be kept for that period and for which the net annual income includes a sum in respect of the higher rate of extensification premium.

In the case of animals which are kept for less than 12 months and for which the net annual income does not include a sum in respect of beef special premium, the net annual income is to be calculated by deducting £82 from the figure in column 3 and then making a pro rata adjustment of the resulting figure.

In the case of animals which are kept for less than 12 months and for which the net annual income includes a sum in respect of beef special premium, the net annual income is to be calculated by first deducting £82 from the figure in column 3, then making a pro rata adjustment of the resulting figure, then adding to that figure the sum of £82 and (where the net annual income includes a sum in respect of extensification premium) the sum of £26 (where the extensification premium is paid at the lower rate) or £37 (where the extensification premium is paid at the higher rate).

(3) This indicates the figure for animals (irrespective of age) which are kept for 12 months. In the case of animals which are kept for less than 12 months a pro rata adjustment of this figure is to be made.

(4) Deduct £22 from this figure in the case of animals for which the net annual income does not include a sum in respect of the premium for offsetting income loss sustained by sheep meat producers (sheep annual premium) provided for in Article 5 of Council Regulation 2467/98.

(5) Deduct £17 from this figure in the case of animals for which the net annual income does not include a sum in respect of sheep annual premium.

(6) Deduct £241 from this figure in the case of land for which the net annual income does not include a sum in respect of the compensatory payment for which producers of arable crops may apply (area payment) provided for in Article 2 of Council Regulation 1765/92 (Article 2 of Council Regulation 1251/99).

(7) Deduct £349 from this figure in the case of land for which the net annual income does not include a sum in respect of area payment.

(8) Deduct £467 from this figure in the case of land for which the net annual income does not include a sum in respect of area payment.

(9) Deduct £240 from this figure in the case of land for which the net annual income does not include a sum in respect of area payment.

(10) Deduct £303 from this figure in the case of land for which the net annual income does not include a sum in respect of area payment.

(11) Deduct £349 from this figure in the case of land for which the net annual income does not include a sum in respect of area payment.

(12) Deduct £241 from this figure in the case of land for which the net annual income does not include a sum in respect of area payment.

AGRICULTURAL HOLDINGS (UNITS OF PRODUCTION) (ENGLAND) ORDER 2000

SI 2000/1984

The Minister of Agriculture, Fisheries and Food, being the Minister designated in relation to England for the purposes of paragraph 4 of Schedule 6 to the Agricultural Holdings Act 1986, and of all other powers enabling him in that behalf, hereby makes the following Order:—

Title commencement and interpretation

1. (1) This Order may be cited as the Agricultural Holdings (Units of Production) (England) Order 2000 and shall come into force on 12th September 2000.

(2) Any reference in this Order to 'the Schedule' is a reference to the Schedule to this Order.

(3) Any reference in this Order to a Community instrument is a reference to that instrument and any amendment of such instrument in force on the date this Order is made.

(4) In this Order:

> 'Council Regulation 2467/98' means Council Regulation (EC) No 2467/98 on the common organisation of the market in sheepmeat and goatmeat;
> 'Council Regulation 1251/99' means Council Regulation (EC) No 1251/99 establishing a support system for producers of certain arable crops;
> 'Council Regulation 1254/99' means Council Regulation (EC) No 1254/99 on the common organisation of the market in beef and veal.

Assessment of productive capacity of land

2. (1) Paragraphs (2) and (3) of this article have effect for the purpose of the assessment of the productive capacity of a unit of agricultural land situated in England, in order to determine whether that unit is a commercial unit of agricultural land within the meaning of subparagraph (1) of paragraph 3 of Schedule 6 to the Agricultural Holdings Act 1986.

(2) Where the land in question is capable, when farmed under competent management, of being used to produce any livestock, crop, fruit or miscellaneous product as is mentioned in any of the entries 1 to 7 in column 1 of the Schedule, then—

(a) the unit of production prescribed in relation to that use of the land shall be the unit specified in column 2 of the Schedule opposite to that entry, and

(b) the amount determined, for the period of 12 months beginning with 12th September 2000, as the net annual income from that unit of production in that period shall be the amount specified in column 3 of the Schedule opposite that unit of production.

(3) Where land capable, when farmed under competent management, of producing a net annual income is designated as set aside land, as is mentioned in entry 8 in column 1 of the Schedule, then—

(a) the unit of production prescribed in relation to that use of the land shall be the unit specified in column 2 of the Schedule opposite to that entry, and

(b) the amount determined, for the period of 12 months beginning with 12th September 2000, as the net annual income from that unit of production in that period shall be the amount specified in column 3 of the Schedule opposite that unit of production.

(4) The Schedule has effect subject to the Notes to the Schedule.

Revocation

3. The Agricultural Holdings (Units of Production) (England) Order 1999 is hereby revoked.

SCHEDULE: PRESCRIBED UNITS OF PRODUCTION AND DETERMINATION OF NET ANNUAL INCOME

Articles 1(2) and 2

Column 1	*Column 2*	*Column 3*
Farming use	Unit of production	Net annual income from unit of production £
1. *Livestock*		
Dairy cows:		
Channel Island breeds	cow	250
Other breeds	cow	308
Beef breeding cows:		
On eligible land under the Hill Livestock (Compensatory Allowances) Regulations 1996	cow	52(1)
On other land	cow	43(1)
Beef fattening cattle (semi-intensive)	head	45(2)

Column 1	Column 2	Column 3
Farming use	Unit of production	Net annual income from unit of production £
Dairy replacements	head	30(3)
Ewes:		
On eligible land under the Hill Livestock (Compensatory Allowances) Regulations 1996	ewe	16(4)
On other land	ewe	18(5)
Store lambs (including ewe lambs sold as shearlings)	head	0.87
Pigs:		
Sows and gilts in pig	sow or gilt	70
Porker	head	1.60
Cutter	head	2.90
Bacon	head	4.10
Poultry:		
Laying hens	bird	0.90
Broilers	bird	0.10
Point-of-lay pullets	bird	0.20
Christmas Turkeys	bird	1.44
2. *Farm arable crops*		
Barley	hectare	112(6)
Beans	hectare	113(7)
Herbage seed	hectare	155
Linseed	hectare	62(8)
Oats	hectare	137(9)
Oilseed rape	hectare	121(10)
Peas:		
Dried	hectare	143(11)
Vining	hectare	237
Potatoes:		
First early	hectare	675
Maincrop (including seed)	hectare	705
Sugar Beet	hectare	288
Wheat	hectare	179(12)
3. *Outdoor horticultural crops*		
Broad beans	hectare	391
Brussels sprouts	hectare	1525
Cabbage, savoys and sprouting broccoli	hectare	1665
Carrots	hectare	2385
Cauliflower and winter broccoli	hectare	1040
Celery	hectare	7545
Leeks	hectare	3070

Column 1		Column 2	Column 3
Farming use		Unit of production	Net annual income from unit of production £
Lettuce		hectare	3950
Onions:			
	Dry bulb	hectare	1305
	Salad	hectare	4263
Outdoor bulbs		hectare	1682
Parsnips		hectare	2591
Rhubarb (natural)		hectare	3750
Turnips and swedes		hectare	1400
4. *Protected crops*			
Forced narcissi		1000 square metres	7225
Forced tulips		1000 square metres	6790
5. *Orchard fruit*			
Apples:			
Cider		hectare	495
	Cooking	hectare	1275
	Dessert	hectare	1360
Cherries		hectare	1085
Pears		hectare	1140
Plums		hectare	1180
6. *Soft fruit*			
Blackcurrants		hectare	840
Raspberries		hectare	2865
Strawberries		hectare	3760
7. *Miscellaneous*			
Hops		hectare	1850
8. *Set-aside*[1]		hectare	26

Notes to the Schedule

Article 2(4)

Note to column 1

(1) For the marketing year 2000–2001 this refers to land which is set-aside under Article 2(3) of Council Regulation 1251/99, except where such land is used (in accordance with Article 6(3) of Council Regulation 1251/99) for the provision of materials for the manufacture within the Community of products not primarily intended for human or animal consumption.

Notes to column 3

(1) Deduct £102 from this figure in the case of animals for which the net annual income does not include a sum in respect of the premium

for maintaining suckler cows (suckler cow premium) provided for in Article 6 of Council Regulation 1254/99.

Add £23 to the figure in column 3 in the case of animals for which the net annual income includes a sum in respect of the lower rate of extensification premium provided for in Article 13 of Council Regulation 1254/99.

Add £45 to the figure in column 3 in the case of animals for which the net annual income includes a sum in respect of the higher rate of extensification premium provided for in Article 13 of Council Regulation 1254/99.

(2) This is the figure for animals which are kept for 12 months.

Deduct £83 in the case of animals which are kept for 12 months and for which the net annual income does not include a sum in respect of the special premium for holding male bovine animals (beef special premium) provided for in Article 4 of Council Regulation 1254/99.

Add £23 to the figure in column 3 in the case of animals which are kept for 12 months and for which the net annual income includes a sum in respect of the lower rate of extensification premium.

Add £45 to the figure in column 3 in the case of animals which would be kept for that period and for which the net annual income includes a sum in respect of the higher rate of extensification premium.

In the case of animals which are kept for less than 12 months and for which the net annual income does not include a sum in respect of beef special premium, the net annual income is to be calculated by deducting £83 from the figure in column 3 and then making a pro rata adjustment of the resulting figure.

In the case of animals which are kept for less than 12 months and for which the net annual income includes a sum in respect of beef special premium, the net annual income is to be calculated by first deducting £83 from the figure in column 3, then making a pro rata adjustment of the resulting figure, then adding to that figure the sum of £83 and (where the net annual income includes a sum in respect of extensification premium) the sum of £23 (where the extensification premium is paid at the lower rate) or £45 (where the extensification premium is paid at the higher rate).

(3) This indicates the figure for animals (irrespective of age) which are kept for 12 months. In the case of animals which are kept for less than 12 months a pro rata adjustment of this figure is to be made.

(4) Deduct £16 from this figure in the case of animals for which the net annual income does not include a sum in respect of the premium for offsetting income loss sustained by sheep meat producers (sheep annual premium) provided for in Article 5 of Council Regulation 2467/98.

(5) Deduct £12 from this figure in the case of animals for which the net annual income does not include a sum in respect of sheep annual premium.

(6) Deduct £216 from this figure in the case of land for which the net annual income does not include a sum in respect of the compensatory payment for which producers of arable crops may apply (area

payment) provided for in Article 2 of Council Regulation 1251/99.

(7) Deduct £268 from this figure in the case of land for which the net annual income does not include a sum in respect of area payment.

(8) Deduct £326 from this figure in the case of land for which the net annual income does not include a sum in respect of area payment.

(9) Deduct £216 from this figure in the case of land for which the net annual income does not include a sum in respect of area payment.

(10) Deduct £309 from this figure in the case of land for which the net annual income does not include a sum in respect of area payment.

(11) Deduct £268 from this figure in the case of land for which the net annual income does not include a sum in respect of area payment.

(12) Deduct £217 from this figure in the case of land for which the net annual income does not include a sum in respect of area payment.

Forms and precedents

STATUTORILY PRESCRIBED FORMS

It is a continuing source of considerable irritation to practitioners that prescribed forms, particularly in respect of applications to the Agricultural Land Tribunal and replies, have not been revised following statutory changes in the law. As a result statutory forms which are long out of date are required to be used which renders them more unintelligible to the recipient than they need to be.

They sometimes give rise to disputes as to the validity of the forms used and add to the costs of litigation.

However, until such time as new forms are prescribed it is presumptuous as well as strictly incorrect to amend and notionally improve the statutorily prescribed forms by bringing them up to date. However, where the current relevant statutory authorities and sections are inserted in substitution for the repealed provisions, such forms, being 'substantially to the like effect' as those statutorily prescribed, will be valid and effective for their purposes.

PART I

Agricultural Land Tribunal

770   Form AH7
Correction: This is Form 4 and not Form 3 of the statutorily prescribed forms applicable for an application for variation or revocation of condition imposed by the Tribunal.

776/777   Form AH11
If, despite the reply made by the landlord to the application by the tenant for approval of long term improvements, the Tribunal grants the tenant's application, the landlord may, if he wishes, carry out the improvements himself. In that event the landlord must, before undertaking the

improvements, give notice within the prescribed period under section 67(5) and he must serve notice in writing on the Tribunal and the tenant that the landlord proposes himself to carry out the improvements. The period now prescribed by the Agricultural Land Tribunals (Rules) Order 1978 is one month.

PART II

Matters arising during tenancy

826   Note 2 to form AH41:
Following the enactment of the Government of Wales Act 1998 and the consequent devolution of certain central Government functions to an elected Assembly for Wales, it is necessary constantly to analyse and update the functions which have devolved. Currently no functions under the Agricultural Holdings Act 1986 have devolved upon the Assembly for Wales with or without Government involvement.

PART III

Termination of tenancy

845   There is a significant omission from the notes to the notice to tenant to remedy breach in Form 2. Paragraph 4 of the notes is defective because the words set out below have been omitted. Substitute the wording on page 845 of the main text read as follows:

What to do if you wish to contest any other question arising under this Notice to remedy
4. If you wish to contest any other question arising under this Notice other than Question (a), (b) or (c), such as whether the time specified in the notice to do work is a reasonable period in which to carry out the work, you should refer the question to arbitration in either of the following ways, according to whether or not you are also at the same time referring question (a), (b) or (c) to arbitration—
(a) If you are referring question (a), (b) or (c) to arbitration, then you must also refer to arbitration at the same time any other questions relevant to this notice which you may wish to dispute.
    To do this, you should include in the notice to your landlord referred to in Note 1 above a statement of the other questions which you require to be determined by arbitration under the Agricultural Holdings Act 1986 (see article 4(1) of the Order).
(b) If you are not referring Question (a), (b) or (c) to arbitration but wish to contest some other question arising under this Notice to remedy,

you may refer that question to arbitration either now on receipt of this notice or later if you get a notice to quit.

To refer the question to arbitration now, you should serve on your landlord *within one month* after the service of this Notice to remedy a notice in writing setting out what it is you require to be determined by arbitration under the Agricultural Holdings Act 1986 (see articles 4(2)(a) of the Order).

Alternatively, you have one month after the service of the Notice to quit within which you can serve on your landlord a notice in writing requiring the question to be determined by arbitration under the 1986 Act (see article 9 of the Order). You will then have three months from the date of service of that notice in which to appoint an Arbitrator by agreement or (in default of such agreement) to make an application under paragraph 1 of Schedule 11 to that Act for the appointment of an Arbitrator. If this is not done by you or your landlord your notice requiring arbitration ceases to be effective (see article 10 of that Order).

852   Case B alternative wording should read:
This notice is given reason that the land which is the subject of this notice is required for a use other than for agriculture:

[state the use in question]

for which permission has been granted on an application made under the enactments relating to town and country planning

or

for which permission under the enactments relating to town and country planning is granted by a general development order by reason only of the fact that the use is authorised by (i) a private or local Act or (ii) an order approved by both Houses of Parliament or (iii) an order made under sections 14 or 16 of the Harbours Act 1964

or

for which a provision that (i) is contained in any Act but (ii) does not form part of the enactments relating to town and country planning deems permission under those enactments to have been granted

or

which the provisions referred to in Case B(c) of Schedule 3 of the Agricultural Holdings Act 1986 deem not to constitute development for the purposes of the enactments relating to town and country planning

or

for which permission is not required under the enactments relating to town and country planning by reason only of Crown immunity.

853   When serving a Case G notice to quit upon the Public Trustee, he requires:
(a) payment of his fee, currently £20; and
(b) completion of his prescribed form; Form NL(1) as set out below.

FORM NL (1)

PUBLIC TRUST OFFICE
AN EXECUTIVE AGENCY

APPLICATION FOR REGISTRATION OF NOTICE AFFECTING LAND
PUBLIC TRUSTEE (NOTICES AFFECTING LAND) (TITLE ON DEATH) REGULATIONS 1995

For explanatory notes see overleaf. *Please type or complete in BLOCK CAPITALS*	For official use only
To: The Public Trustee Public Trust Office PO Box 3010 London WC2B 6JS	**Date of Registration** .... **Registration No.** ....
I .... of .... *(enter name and address of person or firm making application)* apply for registration against the name of the deceased person referred to below of the attached Notice in respect of the land described.	The fee of £ .... accompanies this application. *(Cheques should be made payable to the Public Trust Office).* **Signed** .... **Date** .... **Telephone No.** .... **Reference** ....
Enter name of deceased Forename(s) .... Surname	**Enter details of land to which Notice relates.** *(See explanatory notes).*
Date of Notice .... **Description of Notice** *(see explanatory notes).*	

Explanatory Notes
1   The fee payable is prescribed by the current Public Trustee Fees Order. Please ensure that such fee accompanies your application.

Explanatory Notes – *continued*

2   A practice note explaining the procedure for the keeping of a Register of Notices served under section 18 of the Law of Property (Miscellaneous Provisions) Act 1994 is available from the Public Trust Office free of charge.

3   Separate applications should be made per property except where more than one property is included in the same title.

4   The entry on the Register will be made in the name of the deceased person and will record the details of the land to which the document relates and the date of registration.

5   The date and description of Notice are requested for office purposes only and will not be entered on the Register. Examples of a description of Notice are: Notice to Quit or Notice of Exercise of Option.

6   Please ensure that the Notice to be registered accompanies your application.

7   Acknowledgement of your application will be sent to you indicating the date of registration.

PART IV

Improvements and compensation claims

861   Form AH82 should read: '1986 Act s 32 and s 60'.

PART V

Arbitration

880   Form AH95
The address for The President of The Royal Institution of Chartered Surveyors (Arbitrations Section) is now Surveyors' Court, Westwood Way, Coventry CV4 8JE.

Paragraph B:
The cheque to be enclosed must be for £115 and not £70 as stated.

883   Form AH97
The address for The President of The Royal Institution of Chartered Surveyors (Arbitrations Section) is now Surveyors' Court, Westwood Way, Coventry CV4 8JE.

Paragraph B:
The cheque to be enclosed must be for £115 and not £70 as stated.

Farm Business under the Agricultural Tenancies Act 1995

General introduction

899   Insert:

The Agricultural Tenancies Act 1995 (ATA 1995) has now been in force for over five years. There is still no significant guidance or case authority on any of the specific provisions of the ATA 1995 and, so far as the authors are aware, there have been very few arbitrations under the provisions of the Act. Changes to the text relating to the specific sections of the Act are, therefore, relatively few. Those there are stem from experience of advising on and drafting farm business tenancies and the benefit of further time for reflection since the publication of the eighth edition in November 1996. Experience shows that, along with rent review clauses and clauses concerned with improvements, much of the advice sought continues to be on the question of the interface between the Agricultural Holdings Act 1986 (AHA 1986) and the 1995 Act and the impact that the latter has on the ability of AHA landlords and tenants to manage the AHA land effectively, not only to manage the land, but also to resolve disputes between them (eg relating to succession or the existence or otherwise of an AHA tenancy) by means of the grant of a farm business tenancy. This is much more of a compromise than no tenancy or a tenancy with full security of tenure – an all or nothing situation which produced much litigation.

Noteworthy changes to the general law of landlord and tenant will be covered.

What of the aims of the ATA 1995 five years on – to slow the decline in let land and revitalise the tenanted sector? The CAAV Annual Tenanted Farms Survey for 1999[1] shows a marked increase in the net inflow of new land into the tenanted sector in 1999. With 77,000 previously unlet acres being let on farm business tenancies, the net increase (allowing for losses of land to the tenanted sector) is 61,000 acres. Seventy-five per cent of land in AHA tenancies which terminated were re-let on farm business tenancies. Prior to the coming into force of the 1995 Act, the CAAV surveys showed losses to the tenanted sector of 50,000–70,000 acres a year. At least part of the increase in the period concerned by the survey is the decision by some to cease their own farming operation and let out their land in response to the current agricultural recession, matched by others seeking to expand their enterprises for the same reason.

1   Available from CAAV, Market Chambers, 35 Market Place, Coleford, Gloucester GL16 8AA.

The CAAV survey records the average length of farm business tenancies now to be four years and one month, but for holdings with buildings and a house to be eleven years. Why there has been so little dispute resolution activity is a matter of speculation – particularly amongst lawyers! For short lettings with no security of tenure, the value is simply not there to make the costs of litigating or arbitrating worthwhile. From the tenant's point of view, also, the desire to continue to occupy the land after the end of the current tenancy (and hence preserve the commercial relationship to enable the tenant to negotiate a new term with the landlord) is bound to impact on any decision to pursue disputes. The general move to ADR also means that dispute resolution and decision making is more of a private, unreported affair than it once was. In any situation where it is important to the parties to preserve their commercial relationship mediation is thought by many to come into its own.

PART I

FORMATION OF A FARM BUSINESS TENANCY

Chapter 24

Formation of a farm business tenancy

A. WHAT IS A FARM BUSINESS TENANCY

2. THE SECTION 4 EXCEPTIONS

(2) Succession tenancies—section 4(1)(b)–(d)

907   Delete footnote 1 and substitute:
Concerns have been expressed as to whether an agreed succession following the service of a retirement notice, as opposed to following the death of the previous tenant, falls within the section 4(2) definition. Section 4(2) tests the new tenancy by reference to whether or not it would count as a succession tenancy under the 1986 Act ie would count as one of the two succession 'occasions' under section 37(1)(a) or (b) such as would prevent further successions.

   Section 37(1)(a) refers to directions of the ALT or grants following a direction. Section 37(1)(b) refers only to the new tenancy being granted to a close relative of a tenant who has *died*. There is no direct reference in section 37 to the retirement of a tenant. Section 51 of the 1986 Act states that section 37 will apply to exclude further retirement successions subject to modifications, including references to the date of death being read as references to the date of the giving of a retirement notice. However, section 51 does not operate so as to amend or extend section 37 itself, but merely to state that its terms will apply with modifications to retirement successions. As section 4(2) refers only to section 37 in defining agreed succession for the purposes of the 1995 Act and not to section 51 there is some doubt whether, technically, retirement successions agreed between landlord and tenant can be agreed successions and hence continue to be protected under the 1986 Act. The cautious will obtain a direction from the ALT.

(4) Surrender and re-grant—section 4(1)(f)

910   Add to paragraph (e):
It is not uncommon for a 1986 Act tenant to acquire additional land from his landlord. As part of a negotiated rent review or agreement relating to the payment for improvements, the tenant may 'give' a little if he can take on additional fields. The tenant would much prefer to see such land 'added' to his 1986 Act tenancy and a practice has grown up of landlords asking tenants to accept memorandums of variation 'adding the land to the existing tenancy' and relying on section 4(1)(f). Often the memorandum is prepared by and sent by professional advisors who will be aware that they are effecting a surrender and re-grant. For the reasons set out above, there is risk associated with such an approach although the attitude of the courts to section 4(1)(f) is unknown. One view is that a court would be unlikely, willingly, to interpret the section so as to allow the tenant to lose his security of tenure as a result of such a memorandum, particularly where the other party to the litigation is the landlord who negotiated the 'variation'. However, the cautious will advise that the tenant take the additional land on a farm business tenancy and negotiate the terms to mirror, as closely as possible, the terms of the AHA tenancy. A long fixed term with a break clause to be operated on the termination of the associated AHA tenancy and a rent review formula within Section 9 of the ATA 1995 which tied the rent to the AHA tenancy might be appropriate for a tenancy of small blocks of additional land.

911   Footnote 1:
See also the House of Lords decision of *Bruton v London & Quadrant Housing Trust* [1999] EGCS 90.

3. THE DEFINITION OF A FARM BUSINESS TENANCY

(2) The business conditions

(d) Monitoring compliance

915   Insert:
District Judges have, since the coming into force of the 1995 Act, generally proved amenable to the granting of exclusion orders in cases of uncertainty, most notably where the grazing of horses is concerned (see noter-up to pp 916–917).

(f) Trade or business

916   Insert:
However, the running of a community farm, which is not a profit making enterprise, will not fall within the definition of trade or business as was held in the case of *Secretary of State for Transport v Jenkins, Jenkins, Spence and Taylor* (1999).

(g) Horses

917   Add to sub-paragraph (ii):
An exclusion order should be obtained before the letting goes ahead to exclude the tenancy from the security of tenure (though not from the other) provisions of the 1954 Act.

(4) The notice conditions

(b) The conditions

920   In paragraph (b) delete the word 'from' in the first line and replace with 'at'.

923   At the end of the section insert a new footnote marker 3.

Insert text of new footnote 3:
The view is expressed in Muir Watt and Moss *Agricultural Holdings* (14th edn) p 21) that this view of the width of section 3 is too optimistic and that its terms are confined to cases of surrender and re-grant. It appears, however, that the learned authors accept that section 3 would be available where a fixed term tenancy of more than two years has continued as a result of the operation of section 5 and that the section is only unavailable in respect of a series of fixed term tenancies which expire by effluxion of time.

Certainly, as is stated above, the heading of section 3 would imply that the section was intended to be confined to surrender and re-grant but the only words capable of so confining the section are in section 3(1)(a): that the new tenancy is granted to a person who 'immediately before the grant' was the tenant under a farm business tenancy. On similar wording in the Housing Act 1988 the Court of Appeal has held that a Rent Act 1977 protected tenant lost his protection when, 24 hours after the termination of his Rent Act tenancy, he took a new tenancy because he was not a Rent Act tenant 'immediately before' the grant of the new tenancy (*Bolnore Properties Limited v Cobb* [1996] EGCS 42). This case is relied on by Muir Watt, but it does not answer the case where the parties so arrange matters that the new farm business tenancy commences immediately the old one expires.

B. FORMALITIES

2. FORMALITIES

(1) Contract

924   Add to footnote 2:
An arrangement which fails to comply with section 2(1) may be saved by section 2(5) which expressly preserves the creation and operation of constructive trusts. Such a trust which arises in relation to an agreement, arrangement or understanding is closely akin to, if not indistinguishable from, proprietary estoppel. See *Yaxley v Gott* [1999] 2 EGLR 181, CA. Cf *James v Evans* [2000] EGCS 95 where proprietary estoppel can operate through a constructive trust, section 2(5) may help to save oral agreements or incomplete contracts.

Add to footnote 2:
See *McCausland v Duncan Lawrie Ltd* [1997] 1 WLR 38 – agreements to vary the contract must likewise comply with section 2.

(2) Requirement for a deed

926   Add footnote marker 1a to paragraph (d).

Insert text of footnote 1a:
See however *Parc Battersea Limited v Hutchinson* [1999] EGCS 45 – assignments which are by operation of law as where a sub-tenancy is granted which must last longer than the head tenancy and this operates as an assignment by the head tenant of his interest.

(4) Conveyancing requirements and formalities

928   In paragraph (a), in the penultimate line delete '1996' and replace with '1995'.

(5) Failure to comply with formalities

In the third line delete 'convey' and replace with 'conveying'.

929   Add to footnote 4:
Long v Tower Hamlets London Borough Council [1998] Ch 197.

Add to footnote 6:
Lloyds Bank Plc v Carrick [1996] 4 All ER 630.

PART II
THE TENANCY AGREEMENT

Chapter 26
Implied terms and usual covenants

A. IMPLIED COVENANTS BY THE LANDLORD

935   Add to footnote 7:
Southwark London Borough Council v Mills [1998] 3 EGLR 46.

B. IMPLIED COVENANTS BY THE TENANT

936   At the end of the sentence insert 'A tenant under a fixed term tenancy is liable for both voluntary and permissive waste.[5a]'

Insert text of footnote 5a:
See *Dayani v Bromley London Borough Council* [1999] 3 EGLR 144.

Chapter 28

User covenants

943   Add to footnote 8:
A landlord is entitled to have regard to any impact of the change of use on any business of his own and whether or not the business of the landlord existed at the date of the lease.

Chapter 29

Assignment and sub-letting

944   Add to footnote 3:
Note that a consent 'subject to licence' may be immediately effective. See *Prudential Assurance Co Ltd v Mount Eden Land Ltd* [1997] 1 EGLR, CA and *Next Plc v NFU Mutual* [1997] EGCS 181.

945   Insert at the end of the first paragraph after footnote 2:
An absolute prohibition on assignment in a tenancy to joint tenants will prohibit an assignment from all joint tenants to only one or some of their number. The prohibition may be avoided by the expedient of using a deed of release by the outgoing joint tenants to the remaining tenant or tenants of their interest in the tenancy but there is a significant risk that this would still be held to amount to an assignment.[2a]

Text of footnote 2a:
See the House of Lords decision in *Burton v Camden London Borough Council* [2000] 14 EG 149 where the majority held that this would not work in the context of a statutory bar on assignment in section 91 of the Housing Act 1985 as there was no indication that the word 'assign' in section 91 was not wide enough to cover the situation where a joint tenant 'dropped out'. However, see the strong dissenting speech of Lord Millett.

Insert a new paragraph:
(5) In *Wallace v C Brian Barrett & Son Limited* [1997] 2 EGLR 1 the use by a family company tenant of contractors as its agents to farm a holding consisting of arable land with no dwellings or buildings was held not to be a sharing of occupation by the tenant in breach of an agreement 'not to assign, under let, part with or share possession or occupation of the whole or any part of the holding'. The Court of Appeal pointed out that as the company was only capable of acting through agents, the occupation of an agent, carrying out farming operations on behalf of the tenant, was the occupation of the principal/tenant.

A. FULLY QUALIFIED COVENANTS

947   Add to footnote 5:
See also *Ashworth Frazer Limited v Gloucester City Council* [2000] 12 EG 149, CA.

Chapter 30
Rent and rent review

C. RENT REVIEW FORMULA—EXPRESS TERMS

2. SECTION 9 OPTIONS

(1) General

952   Insert footnote marker '5' at fourth line from bottom of page after the word 'review'.

Insert text of footnote 5:
There is authority that if the machinery (as opposed to the substance) of a rent review breaks down, the court can and should supplement it where the proper construction of the lease is that there should be a rent review for each of the rental periods see *Royal Bank of Scotland plc v Jennings* [1997] 1 EGLR 101, CA where the court found that on a true construction of the lease there was an agreement for a rent review for each period. The lease provided for the landlord only to serve notice but the court would not allow the landlord to frustrate the rent review by refusing to operate the machinery of rent review. (They upheld the decision of the judge at first instance who imposed a mandatory order on the landlord to serve the requisite notice.) See also *Addin v Secretary of State for the Environment* [1997] 1 EGLR 19.

3. EXPRESS RENT REVIEW PROVISIONS NOT WITHIN SECTION 9

(1) Appointment of the third party

960   Add to footnote 1:
In Muir Watt and Moss *Agricultural Holdings* (14th edn), p 52 the view is expressed that no such action would lie. Relying on *Keen v Holland* the authors consider that any other conclusion would be 'contrary to Parliamentary purpose'.

G. PROCEDURE AND THE ARBITRATION

1. TRIGGERING THE RENT REVIEW PROCEDURE

968   Add to footnote 1:
A deeming provision – which provides that a tenant will be deemed to have agreed to a rent level proposed by the landlord in the absence of the service of a counter notice with a set time – will not of itself make time of the essence *Starmark Enterprises Ltd v CPL Distribution Ltd* [2000] EGCS 81 following *Mecca Leisure Limited v Renown Investments (Holdings) Limited* [1984] 2 EGLR 137.

3. DETERMINATION BY AN EXPERT

970   Insert new footnote marker '5a' at end of the section:

Insert text of footnote 5a:
See also *National Grid v M25 Group* [1999] EGCS 2 and noter-up to p 1092 (footnote 1) below.

971   ## 5. EVIDENCE

Delete text and footnotes and substitute:
Evidence of the open market rent is going to come primarily from evidence of comparable lettings. A comparable is any other property which has any evidential contribution to make in the assessment of the rent of the property in question. The weight to be attached to the comparable may, because of differences in material characteristics between the holdings, be limited but that does not prevent it from being a comparable. Likewise, incomplete information will not prevent a property from being a comparable although, again, the weight to be attached to such evidence could be limited as a result.

In *Spath Holme Ltd v Greater Manchester & Lancashire Rent Assessment Committee*[2] it was suggested that lettings under a different code cannot be rejected as inadmissable as comparables simply because of that fact. However, the effect on the rent of different levels of security and the different terms of the letting must be evaluated and taken into account.[3]

The problem of comparables and the hearsay rule has disappeared following the abolition of the hearsay rule in civil cases.[4] However, the case of *Land Securities v Westminster City Council*[5] still presents a problem so far as the use of a previous arbitration award to provide evidence of market value is concerned. It is an award of a tribunal as a matter of fact and is inadmissible to prove any fact before another tribunal.[6]

1   See the Court of Appeal in *Living Walters Christian Centres Limited v Fetlerstorhaugh* [1999] 2 EGLR 1 agreeing with the general observations of the judge at first instance.
2   [1995] 2 EGLR 80.
3   See also Ch 6 in relation to 1986 Act lettings.
4   See Civil Evidence Act 1995.
5   [1993] 1 WLR 286.
6   See *Woodfall* paragraph 8.050 footnote 1 for possible ways around the problem.

971   Add to footnote 2:
See also *Curtis v Chairman of the London Rent Assessment Committee & Others* [1998] 15 EG 120, CA affirming and clarifying the *Spath Homes* decision. *Minja Properties Ltd v Cussins Property Group Plc* [1998] 2 EGLR 52.

Chapter 31

Repairs

D. REMEDIES

1. THE LANDLORD'S REMEDIES

977   Delete the first sentence below (c): 'A landlord is not able to obtain a decree of specific performance to force a tenant to carry out repairs.[2]'

Substitute:
Until recently it was thought that a landlord could not obtain a decree of specific performance against the tenant.[2] However, it would seem that, on the authority of *Rainbow Estates v Tokenhold*[2a] a decree may be available in appropriate circumstances. In the *Rainbow* case there was no power for the landlord to enter to carry out repairs, nor was there a valid forfeiture clause. These factors were considerations in the court's decision to grant specific performance.

Insert text of footnote 2a: [1999] Ch 64.

Add to footnote 5:
CF *Crewe Services & Investment Corporation v Silk* [1998] 2 EGLR 1 where the Court of Appeal drew a distinction between a tenancy which has come to an end (as in *Jones v Herxheimer*) and a continuing tenancy. In the latter case it was held that the diminution in the value of the reversion is the correct test. Further, it was wrong to treat undiscounted costs of repair as a safe guide to diminution in value particularly where there was no finding that the landlord was going to undertake the repairs.

2. THE TENANT'S REMEDIES

978   Third paragraph first sentence delete the words 'unlike a landlord'.

Add to footnote 3: *Joyce v Liverpool City Council* [1996] B 252.

Chapter 32

Other terms

D. RIGHTS OF RE-ENTRY/FORFEITURE CLAUSES

982   Add to footnote 4: see also *Re Palmiero* [1999] 3 EGLR 27.

PART III

TERMINATION OF A FARM BUSINESS TENANCY

Chapter 33

Fixed-term tenancies

A. LETTINGS OF MORE THAN TWO YEARS

989   Add to footnote 1:
In any event, under the Agricultural Holdings Act 1986 it has been held by the Court of Appeal that an agricultural holding which includes a dwelling house does not amount to 'premises let as a dwelling' for the purpose of section 5 of the 1977 Act. The same result would follow for farm business tenancies and, therefore, it will be unnecessary in notices to quit 1995 Act tenancies to include in the notice the prescribed information contained in section 5 of the 1977 Act (see *National Trust for Places of Historic Interest or Natural Beauty v Knipe* [1997] 2 EGLR 9).

Add to footnote 2:
If there is any doubt as to the need to serve a notice (arising, for example, in connection with the validity of the tenancy or the length of the grant (see p 991) a notice may be served 'without prejudice' to any contention by the landlord as to the existence or length of term: *Grammer v Lane* [2000] 04 EG 135, CA.

B. LETTINGS OF TWO YEARS OR LESS

991 Insert a new footnote marker '3a' at end of last line of this section ('expecting to receive'):

Insert footnote 3a:
From the landlord's point of view, if there is a dispute, a notice could be served 'without prejudice' to his contention that it is not needed: see *Grammer v Lane* [2000] 04 EG 135, CA.

D. OPTIONS TO BREAK/EARLY RESUMPTION CLAUSES

993

Insert a new footnote marker '1a' at the end of paragraph (b).

Insert text of footnote 1a:
If there is any doubt over the length of the term (see p 991 above) the landlord should consider the service of a notice in compliance with section 7 'without prejudice' to his position that the term is for two years or less: *Grammer v Lane* [2000] 04 EG 135.

In the paragraph starting 'Other time limits' delete the words:
'The notice exercising the break must itself be clear, unambiguous and, subject to the requirements of section 7, in accordance with the terms of the lease.[3]'

Substitute:
Following the House of Lords decision in *Mannai Investment Co Ltd v Eagle Star Life Assurance Co Ltd*[3] the more rigid rule previously applicable to break notices has gone. The validity or otherwise of a break clause is now tested by the 'standard of commercial construction'. Would a reasonable recipient of the notice in question be left in no reasonable doubt as to what was intended by the notice? In other words, it is the same test as applies to the validity of a notice to quit. The minor error in *Mannai* (specifying the anniversary date of the lease as the 12th rather than the 13th) was not enough to perplex the reasonable recipient.[3a]

Delete text of footnote 3 and substitute:
[1997] 1 EGLR 57. *Hanley v Clavering* [1942] 2 KB 326 was overruled by the House of Lords.

Insert text of new footnote 3a:
cf *Lemmerbell Limited v Britannia LAS Direct Ltd* [1998] 3 EGLR 67, CA where confusion over the identity of the tenant was sufficient to render the notice invalid. See also *Havant International Holdings Ltd v Lionsgate (H) Investment Ltd* [1999] EGCS 144.

Chapter 35

Forfeiture

B. THE RIGHT TO FORFEIT

998   Add to footnote 10:
See also *Re Palmiero* [1999] 38 EG 195.

C. WAIVER OF THE RIGHT TO FORFEIT

1. ACTS AMOUNTING TO WAIVER

1001   Add to footnote 3:
See also *Yorkshire Metropolitan Properties Ltd v Co-operative Retail Services Ltd* [1997] EGCS 57.

D. HOW TO FORFEIT

1. RE-ENTRY

1003   Delete final paragraph of this section and substitute:
To exercise his election to treat the lease as forfeited by court proceedings, the landlord must commence proceedings. Under the Civil Procedure Rules proceedings commence upon the issue by the court of the claim form (whether the action is commenced in High Court or county court).

Delete footnotes 2 and 3.

2. PRELIMINARIES

(2) Other breaches

1005   Add to footnote 5:
See also *Adagio Properties Ltd v Ansari* [1998] EGCS 9.

E. EFFECT OF FORFEITURE

1006   In the first paragraph, line 2 delete: 'when the proceedings are served' and substitute 'when the claim form is issued by the court'.

In the second paragraph, line 1 delete 'after service of court proceedings' and substitute: 'after the issue of the claim form'.

In the third paragraph, line 4 delete 'the service of proceedings' and substitute 'the issue of the claim form'.

Add to footnote 4:
See also *Maryland Estates Ltd v Joseph* [1999] 1 WLR 83.

1007   Insert new footnote marker '9a' at end of last sentence.

Insert text of footnote 9a:
If proceedings are discontinued, the lease is treated as not having been forfeit (*Ivory Gate Ltd v Spetale* [1998] 2 EGLR 44).

F. RELIEF FROM FORFEITURE

5. GUIDELINES FOR THE GRANT OF RELIEF FROM FORFEITURE

1010   Insert:
Even in the case of a deliberate and wilful breach or breaches resulting from the 'sloppy practice' of the tenant the test of whether the tenant is granted relief is still, in essence, an issue of proportionality.[9]

Insert footnote marker '3a' to paragraph (a) of the guidelines laid down in *Rose v Hyman*.

Add to footnote 1:
Note that 'all rent in arrears' for the purposes of relief under section 138 County Courts Act 1984 means the total rent in arrears at the time the court makes its order not just that in arrears at the date of commencement of proceedings (*Maryland Estates Ltd v Bar Joseph* [1998] 2 EGLR 47).
      Note in *Inntrepreneur Pub Co (CPC) v Langton* [1999] EGCS 124 where the tenant's ability to pay the arrears of rent was dependant upon the success of a damages claim against a third party: relief was not granted.

Insert text of footnote 3a:
The court may grant relief upon conditions to be fulfilled within a set period of time. Although extensions to that timetable may be granted, the court could run out of patience and order delivery up of the holding to the

landlord. See *Crawford v Clarke* [2000] EGCS 33 where the tenant's application for a third extension of time to complete repairs – required because the builders had left the site following the tenant's failure to pay them – was refused even though the works were nearly complete.

Insert text of footnote 9:
See *Mount Cook Land Ltd v Hantley & Others* [2000] EGCS 26.

1012   Add to footnote 8:
Barrett v Morgan [2000] 06 EG 165.

Chapter 37

Fixtures and buildings

1021   Add to footnote 3:
See also *Re Palmiero* [1999] 3 EGLR 27.

PART IV

FIXTURES AND COMPENSATION FOR IMPROVEMENTS

Chapter 38

Compensation for improvements

B. TENANT'S IMPROVEMENTS

1. PHYSICAL IMPROVEMENTS AND ROUTINE IMPROVEMENTS

1026/27   Add to footnote 7:
Delete sentence at bottom of p 1026 and top of p 1027:
'It connotes the provision by the tenant of something which has added value to (ie improved) the land itself.'

Substitute:
It connotes the provision by the tenant of some physical item or works carried out on the holding. Whether or not such an improvement adds value goes to the question of compensation rather than the issue of definition.

2. INTANGIBLE ADVANTAGES

1030   Delete the text of footnote 4 and replace with:
See reg 11 of the Dairy Produce Quotas Regulations 1997.

Add to footnote 7:
See also *Harries v Barclays Bank* [1997] 2 EGLR 14 in the Court of Appeal and *Swift v Dairywise Farms Ltd* [2000] 1 All ER 320.

C. ENTITLEMENT TO COMPENSATION

1032   Insert a new footnote marker '2' at the end of the final sentence of the second paragraph (a) (four lines from the bottom of the page).

Insert text of footnote 2:
See *Grammer v Lane* [2000] 04 EG 135, CA.

D. CONSENT OF THE LANDLORD

1034   Add to footnote 3:
See the case of *Prudential Assurance Co Ltd v Mount Eden Land Ltd* [1997] 1 EGLR, CA, consent given 'subject to licence' immediately effective. See also *Next plc v NFU Mutual* [1997] EGCS 181.

1035   In line 6 of paragraph (e) delete 'the Dairy Produce Quotas Regulations 1994' and substitute 'the Dairy Produce Quotas Regulations 1997'.

Chapter 39

Dispute resolution

B. ARBITRATION

1. GENERAL

1057   Add new footnote marker '9a' after words 'Arbitration Act 1996' in final line of page.

Insert text of footnote 9a:
It should not be forgotten that the court has an inherent jurisdiction to stay which can be used in circumstances outside those considered in section 9.

See recently *Al-Naimi v Islamic Press Agency Inc* (2000) Times 16 March, CA.

1058   Add to footnote 1:
See the House of Lords decision in *Inco Europe Ltd v First Choice Distributions* [2000] on the issue of appeals to the Court of Appeal from the grant or refusal of a stay.

Add to footnote 4:
An application to set aside default judgment, applying (unnecessarily) for leave to defend and applying for consequential directions do not amount to steps in the proceedings to answer the substantive claim.

B. ARBITRATION

11. REPLACEMENT OF THE ARBITRATOR

(3) Removal of the Arbitrator

1070   First para (a) At the end of sentence add new footnote marker '1a'.

Insert text of footnote 1a:
See the guidance of the Court of Appeal in *Locobail (UK) Ltd v Bayfield Properties Ltd* [2000] QB 451 as to the issue of bias for judges. Note also the Human Rights Act 1998 (in force 2 October 2000) and the right to a fair trial contained in art 6. This may extend to compulsory (though not voluntary) references to arbitration.
See also *Laker Airways v FLS Aerospace Ltd* [1999] and *Andrews v Bradshaw* (1999) Times, 11 October, CA.

C. ALTERNATIVE DISPUTE RESOLUTION

5. DETERMINATION BY AN EXPERT

1092   Insert a new footnote marker '1' at the end of the section.

Insert text of footnote 1:
See *National Grid v M25 Group* [1999] EGCS 2 where the extent of the expert's remit was looked at in the context of a rent review: it was held that where an expert was appointed to determine the rent, matters of construction relating to the rent review provision were not necessarily within the 'exclusive remit' of the expert and could, therefore, be challenged in the courts or the subject of a preliminary hearing in the court.

PART VI

MISCELLANEOUS

Chapter 40

Services of notices or documents; powers of limited owners; estimation of best rent; Crown land

A. SERVICE OF NOTICES OR DOCUMENTS

1. POSTING

1096   Add to footnote 4:
See also (in the context of section 196(3) of the Law of Property Act 1925) *Kinch v Bullard* [1999] 1 WLR 423. Notice sufficiently served if left at last known place of abode or address.